No Way Home

One War - Two Sisters

Elisabeth Dunleavy

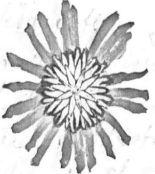

First edition independently published in the United Kingdom 2023.

A CIP catalogue record of this book is available from the British Library.

ISBN (Hardcover): 978-1-7395024-0-9
ISBN (Paperback): 978-1-7395024-2-3 (B&W)
Typesetting design Matthew J Bird

For further information about this book, please contact the author at:
lis@edun-writer.com

Dedicated to
Christa-Maria Cross (née Ciba) and Ursula Ciba,
with heartfelt gratitude, admiration and love.

Contents

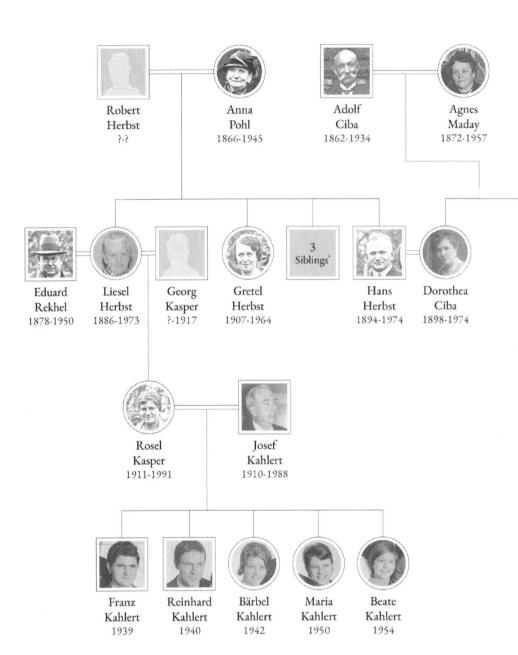

Robert
Herbst
?-?

Anna
Pohl
1866-1945

Adolf
Ciba
1862-1934

Agnes
Maday
1872-1957

Eduard
Rekhel
1878-1950

Liesel
Herbst
1886-1973

Georg
Kasper
?-1917

Gretel
Herbst
1907-1964

3
Siblings*

Hans
Herbst
1894-1974

Dorothea
Ciba
1898-1974

Rosel
Kasper
1911-1991

Josef
Kahlert
1910-1988

Franz
Kahlert
1939

Reinhard
Kahlert
1940

Bärbel
Kahlert
1942

Maria
Kahlert
1950

Beate
Kahlert
1954

*Maria
Herbst
1887-?

*Georg
Herbst
1889-?

*Max
Herbst
1899-?

Josef
Jurettko
1862-1898

Martha
Halamuda
1866-1930

Arthur
Ciba
1895-1969

Margarete
Jurettko
1894-1993

Alfred
Jurettko
1891-1915

Josef Ernst
Jurettko
1890-1946

Elisabeth
Frank
1895-1946

Paul
Jurettko
1889-1937

Katarina
Rumpoldt
1884-?

Ursula
Ciba
1925-2020

Christa-Maria
Ciba
1926-2020

Bernard
Cross
1920-2000

Jochen
Jurettko
1931-2004

Günter
Jurettko
1926-?

Michael
Cross
1955

Margarete
Cross
1956

Monica
Cross
1957

Elisabeth
Cross
1959

Barbara
Cross
1962

André
Jurettko
1962

"There's no diary" you said.
"Not like your father, who wrote everything down.
What the weather was like. Why he went into town.
"No, nothing like that from me," you said.
Nothing to say what your life had been like,
When you slept on a cart in the darkness at night,
On the road, frightened and living in dread.
Those memories packed up inside your head,
And kept in your heart for years on end.
No talking or telling could settle those thoughts,
Nor remove them, nor serve to mend,
A life derailed by war.
Yet here we are, some eighty years later,
Your words in my hands, written pencil on paper,
In a drab, brown notebook, like one used at school,
Revealing your secrets, your strength shining through,
This woman, my mother, whom I never knew.
Learning about you, though you're not here to ask.
Translating your diary - a long, challenging task.
It's something I simply know I must do,
To hear, in your words, what happened to you.

Prologue

I remember the day in 2002 when my mother handed me my father's diaries. We were on the landing of her house in Warwickshire. She wore her usual navy-blue slacks, quilted gilet, a Liberty silk scarf around her neck and her worn-down navy crocs. She came out of the study, the smallest of the bedrooms, offering me three, hardback page-a-day volumes.

"There's nothing like that from me," she said.

I barely registered her words, too focused on the diaries in my hand. I flipped through the pages of my father's 1943 volume, assuming my mother meant she had no physical diaries. She never spoke about her wartime experiences in Germany, so I left it at that.

In more recent years, when I became curious enough to ask, my mother preferred the peace of her own home, rather than my noisy and chaotic house, for conversations about her German family history - my German family history. We sat in her living room, she in her Ercol-style chair, and I, to her left, on the dusky pink velvet sofa. She told me about the familiar people in the photographs around the room - Oma Ciba on the wall, her Mutti on the bookshelf and Oma Jurettko on the windowsill. She smiled and nodded in recollection as she spoke of the special relationship she had had with her paternal grandmother, Oma Ciba; or the times she went ice-skating on the lake in winter with her Mutti and sister, Ursula. I loved the sound of my maternal great grand mother's maiden name – Halamuda! Punchy and exotic, not a German or Polish sounding name at all! However, when I asked about what happened to her during and after the war, reluctant to talk, she shook her head and stared into the distance with an absent gaze. Her answers were limited, and she wouldn't go into any detail. She couldn't bring herself to recall those memories and kept them locked away.

"Ach! Why would anyone be interested in those terrible years?" She asked in frustration before changing the subject.And never any mention of a diary.

Over the years, I treasured the times when she did tell me more about what happened in 1945. Anything longer than ten minutes seemed to upset her, and she didn't want to go on.

Gradually, I pieced together her account and wrote a summary of the harrowing journey she made between November 1944 and December 1945. By the time my mother died in October 2020, I had managed to collate some notes, photographs, and stories about our family and her life before the war in Gleiwitz, her hometown on the German-Polish border. But without more details, how much of a story would I have to pass on? My aunt Ursula, or Tante Ursula, as I knew her, lived in Frankfurt am Main, Germany. She had a profound influence on my life, despite living in a different country. I remember visits to Frankfurt as a teenager, looking at photo albums of Ursula's life from her birth to her late teens. A story in pictures, yet these albums had a story of their own and I was amazed they existed at all. At the time, I was only bold enough to ask who was who in the array of relatives resting on the table in front of me.

While looking through these albums together, Ursula alluded to a diary she had written in 1945. How I wish I had been more interested and curious about that! It wasn't until after her death in April 2020, my sister and I found her diary while clearing her flat in Frankfurt, which we brought back to England.

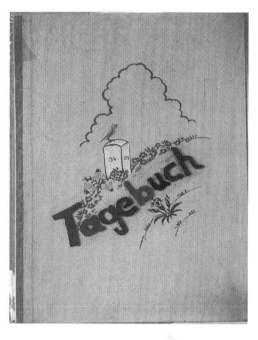

Once back home, I became keeper of the diary. This most precious thing - priceless and far more valuable to me than any jewellery, china, crystal, clothes or furniture we brought back - was a thing of beauty. The hard cover was personalised by Ursula with watercolour floral detail and the word 'Tagebuch' placed diagonally from bottom left to top right in letters individually cut from soft, coloured leather. It was so typical of Ursula to have crafted this attention to detail on what would otherwise have been a plain, lined notebook. I kept it in a stiff, white A4 envelope; the kind in which hefty legal documents might be sent and put it in a plastic bag before laying it in my bedside drawer. Like a diligent archivist, Ursula's diary was only to be touched with freshly washed and dried hands, laid on a clean table with absolutely no food or half-finished cups of tea in sight.

In this way, I sat many times, turning the pages, peering at the words written there, peeking into hidden envelopes filled with newspaper cuttings, photographs or a handmade card. As I leafed through the book, a turned page might reveal another keepsake - a letter, a cinema ticket, a pressed flower or a map – carefully placed and relating to what was written there.

Only able to read the occasional word - Ursula's handwriting so unfamiliar I couldn't work out what the German words were - I asked my mother if she would read it to me. I went to see her, one afternoon in June 2020, hoping she could translate a few pages at a time for me. She would be able to read her sister's cursive handwriting and explain the nuances of the German language.

As she sat in her chair, the one she always used to sit in, I leaned forward from my seat on the pink velvet sofa and handed her the diary wrapped in its paper and plastic bag protection.

"What's this?" She asked, already feeling through the packaging and about to answer her own question.

"Ursula's?" She looked at me and pulled the diary out of the bag onto her lap. I nodded in reply.

"She wrote this?"

Gazing down, she turned the closed book in her hands, front to back then front again, touching the leather letters with her fingertips.

She looked up at me.

"I've never seen this before," she said, handing me the diary.

What must she have felt in that moment? Holding memories of that year, 1945, in her hands, heavy like a stone.

I opened it at the page I had been trying to read, hesitantly pronouncing the words, before offering it back to her in the hope she would continue.

She read the two pages from 18 - 20th January, before closing the diary on her lap.

"I don't want this," she said, staring beyond me through the window into the garden, as she handed it back.

"You have it."

A few months later we were sorting and clearing again; this time, my mother's house in Warwickshire. After she died, we spent several weeks painstakingly going through her home, each of my siblings in a different room, opening drawers and cupboards, bringing items out for the difficult 'cherish, charity shop or chuck' decision, each of us finding sentimental value in things not seen since our childhoods and each of us in a different state of readiness to claim or let them go.

Whilst flicking through books and rifling through boxes in her bedroom, I discovered two drab, brown notebooks in a shoebox at the bottom of her wardrobe, the back cover missing from one and so shabby they might easily have been put in the 'chuck' pile.

They were diaries and letters from 1945, written sporadically, in her instantly recognisable German handwriting, some entries in pen, others in pencil.

Her diaries!

The very thing she had told me didn't exist, all those years ago!

Had she forgotten about them? Had she lied to me? No, surely not! She would never have lied to me! Why didn't she tell me?

In the years since then, I have often been puzzled and upset by this. She led me to believe she hadn't written any diaries and yet, here I am, leafing through and translating what she had told me didn't exist. How could that be? The truth is, it wasn't so much what she had said as what I had heard, which, with a little more curiosity, would have made all the difference.

"There's nothing like that from me." She had said, and she was right. Her diaries are nothing like the gentle, parochial, descriptions of life in Staffordshire my father had written about in his diaries, as a young man.

Listen. Be curious. Ask the right questions while you still can.

Author Notes

Throughout the diary entries, text written in italics are my words rather than Ursula's or Christa-Maria's.

Christa-Maria used a letter format for some of her diary entries. These letters were not sent.

Letters that were sent and received are given a shaded background.

Christa-Maria could speak English, so there are instances, in the diaries, where an English word was used; or a mix of English and German was used to create a made-up word they both understood.

The pressed flowers on the title and dedication page were found between the pages of Christa-Maria's diary. They are seventy-eight years old!

CHAPTER ONE

A Peaceful Life in Gleiwitz

Gleiwitz, Hotel Schlesischer Hof

Come with me. I want to show you something. This is where my mother was born. Look! Up there! In that third-floor apartment, along the Klodnitz canal, above the Schlesischer Hof Hotel on the corner of Wilhelm Strasse and Klodnitz Strasse in Gleiwitz, Upper Silesia, Germany. It was there my widowed, great grandmother, Martha Jurettko (née Halamuda) lived, taking in lodgers to make ends meet. It was there her daughter, Margarete, and sons Paul, Josef and Alfred lived, and it was there Artur Josef Valentin Ciba arrived looking for lodgings in 1923.

Artur and Margarete married on 29th July 1924 at the All-Saints church in Gleiwitz. They lived with Martha for the next few years, during which time my aunt, Ursula Dorothea, was born in April 1925 and my mother, Christa-Maria Agnes, in November 1926.

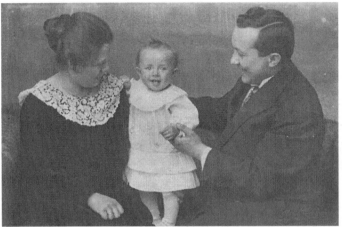

Ursula with her parents on her 1st birthday 12th April 1926.

Christa-Maria on her 1st birthday 29th November 1927.

Artur Ciba's heart would have swelled with pride when, in 1928, his young family moved to a modern apartment at 5, Paul Keller Strasse, Gleiwitz.

The second-floor apartment boasted three bedrooms, a bathroom, kitchen, living room, dining room and a study! Artur Ciba was a senior government tax inspector and provided well for his family. The fine solid

wood furniture, oil paintings, a radiogram and a piano exuded elegance, while the curtains, thick rugs and plump featherbeds promised comfort and cosy warmth during the cold Gleiwitz winters.

Artur was an accomplished pianist and lover of finesse and quality, seen in the exacting standards he held for his family, his appearance and possessions. His mantra 'Alles auf ort und Stelle' meant a place for everything and everything in its place; so that you could find things blind or in the dark, should you need to. He had a lighter side too, joking and laughing with his young relative, Franz Kahlert, who nicknamed him 'Onkel Kohlekasten' - Uncle Coal Scuttle, because his jet-black hair and dusky olive complexion reminded him of a black coal scuttle that might have stood next to the stove. Artur was a collector of stamps and coins, which he kept in beautifully presented albums. Being diabetic meant he was not called up to fight in either the First or Second World War.

Ursula and Christa-Maria grew up in a strict, yet loving, Catholic household. Margarete gave up her job as a telephone operator to become Mutti (mother) and a homemaker. Skilled in baking, cooking, needlework and knitting, she occupied herself with embroidery during evenings of conversation or listening to the radiogram in the sitting room.

As the seasons came and went, Mutti harvested, preserved and stored fruits, vegetables and nuts grown in the communal allotment garden or foraged on family walks in the nearby forest. By the time autumn had become winter, the cellar shelves were full of Kilner jar preserves and pickles - green beans, cherries, cucumbers and plums. A large earthenware pot, covered with a well-fitting plate and weighed down with a small rock, held Mutti's finely sliced white cabbage and salt that would ferment to become sauerkraut, ready in time for Christmas.

The family went to Mass every Sunday morning at the All-Saints Church in Gleiwitz, often followed by services of benediction and rosary devotions later in the day. On religious feast days and holy days of obligation, Ursula and Christa-Maria would take part in celebratory processions, singing hymns and carrying candles, flowers or banners. Morning and night-time prayers were a daily ritual, as were prayers of gratitude before and after meals. They ate their meals together at a finely laid table, covered with one of Mutti's intricately embroidered cloths, with Vater (father) at the head.

While Mutti cleared up after their dinner, Ursula and Christa-Maria would listen attentively to their Vater. His lessons and wisdom extolled the virtues of a strong work ethic, self-discipline and deep faith.

As young girls, with only nineteen months between them, Ursula and Christa-Maria were often mistaken for twins, seen here in 1935, dressed in the same handmade clothes, sewn by their Mutti or the visiting dressmaker, Fräulein Mellich. Twice a year, Fräulein Mellich would stay for a week to make the girls a 'capsule wardrobe' for the coming season. Mutti advised on style, design and fabrics for Ursula and Christa-Maria's clothes and kept a watchful eye as she embroidered her own monogram, 'MC', on pillowcases, napkins and antimacassars for the sitting room chairs. Another needlewoman, Fräulein Vanas, came to launder, press and mend the white linen - table cloths, napkins and bedding. She would share the spare bedroom with Fräulein Mellich for the duration of their stay.

Ursula and Christa-Maria shared a bedroom and spent their time together as youngsters. They read books, played with dolls, teddy bears and traditional handmade wooden 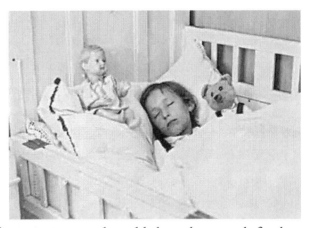 toys. Christa-Maria's favourite toy was the teddy bear she named after her cousin, Günter. She would take her teddy bear to bed every night and look a picture of innocence; her long brown hair plaited and resting on the pillow, snuggled down under her featherbed, clean and cosy after a bath shared with her sister.

Christa-Maria's 3ʳᵈ birthday 29ᵗʰ November 1929.

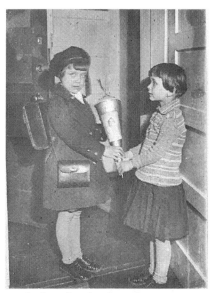

When Ursula started school in 1931 at the Catholic Marien Convent in Gleiwitz, Christa-Maria gave her a 'Schultüte' - a German family tradition of presenting a large, decorated cardboard cone filled with treats and useful things for the first day at school. Receiving the cone as she prepared to leave the house, Ursula looked quite the new pupil- from her beret-covered head to her perfectly polished shoes, her leather satchel on her back and purse worn across her body.

Oma Ciba with Pips, the budgerigar.

Deprived of her sister's company, Christa-Maria spent more time with her paternal Grandmother, Oma Ciba, whom she adored and called 'Sternschen' because she had a twinkle in her eye and brought a sparkle to even the most ordinary pastimes. Sometimes Oma let 'Pips', their pet budgerigar, out of his cage to perch on her out-stretched forefinger, much to Christa-Maria's delight. They read together - 'Max und Moritz' or 'Struwelpeter.'

The family had a white cat named 'Prinzessin Suleika Von Sidi bel Abes'. After Sidi had had a wash, she was placed, wet and disgruntled, in an open, low-heat oven where she purred and preened until she was dry

They played the drawing/rhyme game, a character made from a circle, square and triangle appearing on the page. Santa Clause's single line lantern house, where you were not allowed to lift your pencil off the page, was a favourite at Christmas.

Christa-Maria joined Ursula at school in 1933. In May 1935, the sisters made their First Holy Communion, in the chapel of their convent school. They wore white dresses with a floral wreath on their heads and held a symbolic candle, white lace handkerchief and prayer book. The crocheted cape over their shoulders, was made by Frau Trautmann, a family friend who thought of Ursula and Christa-Maria as her adopted daughters, since she and Herr Trautmann only had two sons. Herr Trautmann worked with Artur Ciba at the tax office in Gleiwitz

Christa-Maria (seated) and Ursula, on their First Holy Communion Day, May 1935.

Christian festivals, milestones and birthdays were celebrated with reverence and attention to every detail in the Ciba household; some traditions that still exist now, generations later.

Ursula's 9th birthday April 1934. Ursula sits next to her friend, Trautel Lamla with white bows, at the head of the table.

'Faschingsfeier' 1935, the carnival celebration prior to the Lenten season of fasting.

Seated left to right: Oma Herbst (Anna), Tante Liesel (Elisabeth Reichel), Mutti (Margarete Ciba), Ursula (behind wine glasses), Christa-Maria (behind vase of flowers).

Standing left to right: Gretel Herbst, Georg Schnyder (Gretel's future husband) Rosel Kahlert,

Eduard Reichel, Vater (Artur Ciba), Maria Pech (née Herbst)

During these peaceful years, before the rise of Hitler's National Socialist Party and the Third Reich, the Ciba family lived an idyllic life in Gleiwitz; a close-knit community, surrounded by friends and family. After church on Sundays, the family would often stroll in the parks and gardens, meeting friends and neighbours at a park bench or at Miethoff's, the delicious chocolatier and confectioners, conveniently owned by Onkel Edi (Eduard Reichel). The anticipation of peering into the window, eagerly searching for a choice of confection was matched only by the joy of entering the shop, buying it, and carrying the ribbon-tied box home for afternoon coffee with friends.

Allotment garden, Gleiwitz, 1934.

Front Row - Left to Right. Margarete Ciba, Christa-Maria Ciba, unknown woman, Agnes Ciba, Oma Herbst, (Anna, née Pohl) Liesel Reichel. (née Herbst, widowed Kasper)

Back Row - Left to Right. Artur Ciba, Eduard Reichel, Rosel Kasper, Dorothea Herbst (née Ciba) Hans Herbst, Gretel Herbst, Ursula Ciba.

The family connection between the Ciba, Reichel, Kahlert and Herbst families living in Gleiwitz, kept them close in what were to become tough times.

Christmas was a time of great preparation and excitement. In late November or early December, Ursula and Christa-Maria loved the earthy woodland smells and leaves rustling underfoot as they gathered small fir tree branches, pinecones, lichen and moss from the woods to make an advent wreath, placing four red candles around the edge. The ritual candle lighting, to mark the passing of weeks until Christmas, happened each Sunday afternoon after 'Kaffee und Kuchen'; a German tradition serving freshly made coffee from a fine China coffee pot into fine China cups served with slice of Streusel or Mohnkuchen (poppyseed cake) on fine China plates. Mutti and the girls would sing Christmas songs gathered round the piano, while Vater played 'O, Tannenbaum' and other carols. Excitement grew on 6th December, St Nicholas' feast day, when Ursula and Christa-Maria, reverential hands folded in prayer, welcomed Santa Claus (Onkel Josef in elaborate costume) through the door of their apartment. With a long, thin pipe and bag of clementines and walnuts, only for good children, 'Santa' played his part in this Ciba custom during the Christmas preparations. In the week before Christmas there was the traditional baking of Pfefferkuchen, Lebkuchen and Stollen; the girls eager to mix, measure and ultimately decorate the biscuits on Christmas Eve. Vater brought home a live carp, left swimming in the bath until it was time to cook the Christmas Eve dinner - grilled carp, homemade sauerkraut and potatoes served with Sekt (champagne) in elegant crystal glasses.

The Christmas tree, always a large, real fir tree, was put up on Christmas Eve and secretly decorated by Mutti and Vater. Individual strands of silver lametta were meticulously draped over the branches, under Vater's supervision. Real beeswax candles were held in place with brass pinecone-shaped clips to complete the perfectly proportioned tree.

After Christmas Eve dinner, Ursula and Christa-Maria helped Mutti tidy up while Vater lit all the candles on the tree in the sitting room, holding the door open and ushering them in, as they returned from the kitchen.

Left to right, Oma Jurettko (Martha), Vater, baby Ursula and Mutti in 1925.

On seeing the shimmering tree, their gasps of delight gave way to a closer inspection of the presents underneath, crouching down to feel the size and shape to guess what might be inside. They sang carols in the twinkling candlelight round the piano. Ursula and Christa-Maria took turns to play, hoping for Vater's approval of the progress they had made that year.

Onkel Josef (Jurettko), Tante Elly with son Jochen 1932.

Left to right - Oma Jurettko, Vater, Mutti, Onkel Josef with Baby Christa-Maria, Tante Elly, Onkel Paul with Ursula on his lap. Christmas Day, 1926.

Onkel Josef, Tante Elly and Jochen, less often Onkel Paul from Breslau, were there to share dinner and exchange gifts before walking through the snow-covered streets to Midnight Mass at All-Saints Church. Celebrations continued throughout the next day with a goose and spiced red cabbage for lunch, taken at an elaborately laid table, decorated by Mutti and her girls.

In the remaining winter holiday, Ursula and Christa-Maria often went ice skating on a local frozen lake. They wore leather lace-up boots with steel blades, skirts and woollen tights on their skinny fawn-like legs.

Enjoying the freedom and exhilaration of the freezing air on their faces, they raced or pirouetted around each other on the ice.

Sometimes, Mutti came on the ice too; skating three abreast, their arms crossed over each other, a synchronised swing of legs to right and left, propelled them around the lake.

If not skating, the snowy winters would see the girls sledging with Mutti and Tante Dorchen.

Christa-Maria would sit keenly at the front of their traditional wooden sledge, rope in hand, ready to go; while Ursula stood uncertainly at the back with Mutti, not sure she even wanted to sit on it, let alone go anywhere. Such was the difference in their personalities.

As the harsh, snowy winters gave way to spring, the family went for picnics with Oma and Opa Ciba, Tante Dorchen and Onkel Hans, and cycle rides in the forest nearby. Tante Dorchen taught the girls to ride bikes, which they loved. Cycling gave them independence, as teenagers, to go to the local lido in Richtersdorf, where they spent many a summer day with friends at the Ciba's poolside cabin.

August 1928, Neustadt, Upper Silesia. Ursula with Tante Dorchen, Oma and Opa Ciba, reclining.

June 1931, Stadtwald, Gleiwitz.

August 1939. Ursula and Christa-Maria leaving their
apartment at 5, Paul Keller Strasse, Gleiwitz to go swimming.

The family spent summer holidays in the late 1930s at the beach in
Bodenhagen, on the Baltic Sea, renting a log cabin and hiking in the Stolowe Mountains bordering Poland and the Czech Republic or visiting the spa towns Bad Kudowa and Kolberg with beautiful botanical gardens and churches.

Artur captured these trips on camera and cine film. During the 1930s, the rise of Hitler's National Socialist Party meant families were encouraged to film and record their lives, highlighting Germany as a wholesome and prosperous nation.

Bodenhagen - In the waves of the Baltic Sea, 1939.

Heuscheuer, 1936.

August 1935, Richtersdorf Lido, Gleiwitz.

1936 Bad Kudowa, Germany. Now Kudowa-Zdrój, Poland.

In 1938, Ursula and Christa-Maria had to leave their Catholic convent school and attend a state school, The Eichendorff Oberschüle, because Vater held a government office as a tax inspector - such was the Nazi party's control over the lives of ordinary German citizens.

As the Nazi campaign against the Jewish people gathered momentum, terrible attacks on Jewish synagogues and businesses took place on the night of 9/10th November 1938. Known as Kristallnacht, it referred to the litter of broken glass twinkling on the streets after the pogroms and destruction of Jewish property all over Germany. There was a synagogue in Gleiwitz, close to where the Ciba family lived.

A walkway between apartment buildings leading to it was known, locally, as Jewish Alley. The synagogue and Jewish businesses were destroyed that night.

The persecution of the Jewish people continued - Christa-Maria remembers classmates being at school one day and not the next, never to be seen again. As a young boy, Franz Kahlert, Rosel's eldest son, remembers hearing anguished cries on the street below their apartment, believing it to be someone hit by a tram. Only as an adult, visiting Gleiwitz after an absence of seventy-three years, did he realise the truth; the screams were from Jewish families being rounded up and forced to leave their homes; his family had lived in the heart of the Jewish quarter in Gleiwitz and Onkel

Edi had been a block warden[1] for that area during the Second World War. (WW2)

The Kahlert Family - Rosel and three young children Franz, Reinhard and Bärbel - left Gleiwitz on 19th January 1945. Franz recalls seeing emaciated Auschwitz-Birkenau prisoners on The Death March [2] along the streets of Gleiwitz, as he made his way to the station, accompanied by Onkel Edi. Rosel's mother, Liesel, and Oma Herbst (Anna) stayed behind because Oma Herbst was too frail to travel.

Were Ursula and Christa-Maria aware of what was happening in Germany as they were growing up? There is no way of knowing what they knew of the atrocities being perpetrated in the name of the German people.

Gleiwitz was in Upper Silesia, Southeast Germany, close to the border with Poland. Over the centuries, borders had changed and been redrawn many times. Upper Silesia had been ruled by the Polish Piast Dynasty, the Kingdom of Bohemia, The Habsburg Empire, Prussia and, since 1872, the German Empire. After the First World War (WW1) and the Silesian Uprisings in 1919 - 1921, the region was divided between Germany and Poland under the terms of the Treaty of Versailles, after a referendum in

---

1 A block warden was a civilian position, typically appointed by local Nazi party officials to distribute propaganda, enforce curfews and blackout regulations as well as keeping a level of surveillance and control over everyday life during WW2, reporting suspicious activity to the authorities.

2 The Death March refers to the forced movement of up to 60,000 Auschwitz-Birkenau prisoners under Nazi guard, to railway junctions over 60 kms away. Already weak from exposure, hunger and abuse they were made to walk west in freezing conditions, wearing nothing more than striped camp issue clothes. Those who were too weak and couldn't keep up were shot. From the railway junctions they travelled to new camps in the Reich interior, keeping them on German territory to be used as forced labour in the months ahead. The camps they left behind were burned or demolished and any evidence of war crimes, including documents, were destroyed. Some prisoners arrived at the four hastily constructed, yet unfinished, concentration sub-camps on the outskirts of Gleiwitz in January 1945, starving, emaciated, barely alive.

1921. The border between the two countries ran through the middle of Upper Silesia.

Its people were proud and fervently religious, mainly Roman Catholic. Each of its diverse population groups - Jews, ethnic Germans, German-speaking Silesians, Polish and Czechs - had a strong culture and sense of identity, creating tension in the years before WW2.

An industrialised area, Gleiwitz was an important centre for coal mining and steel production, supplying German industries since the 1900s.

The Gleiwitz Incident took place on 31st August 1939, when Ursula was 14 years old, and Christa-Maria was 12. The radio mast in Gleiwitz was destroyed and its operator murdered by German soldiers dressed in Polish uniforms, who then broadcast in Polish, urging Poles in the area to revolt against the Germans. This was one of several 'false flag' attacks staged to appear as Polish aggression, known as Operation Himmler, and was used as the pretext for the invasion of Poland on 1st September 1939 - the beginning of WW2.

In June 1941, the German invasion of the Soviet Union, Operation Barbarossa, resulted in the wounding and death of millions, both military personnel and innocent Russian civilians. Despite this invasion, Hitler did not make gains on Soviet Territory due to poor strategic planning and German underestimation of the severity of a Russian winter. When the Russian Army reached Germany in 1945, the memory of the German brutality towards Russians was still strong. The Russian soldiers were seeking revenge and retaliation for German atrocities committed against the Russian people. Consequently, there was heightened fear of rape, torture and murder amongst German civilians, particularly for young women like Ursula and Christa-Maria, when the Russian army invaded Germany in January 1945.

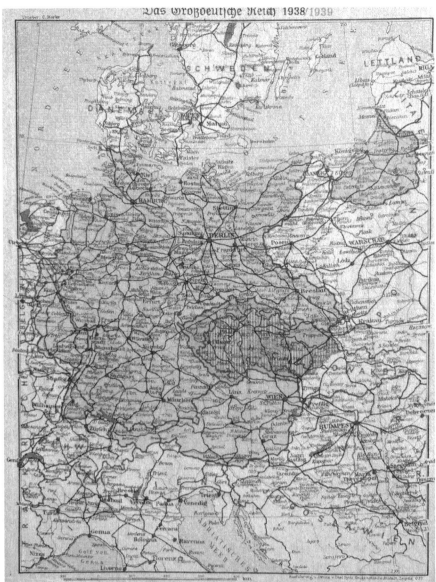

Pale grey - Greater German Reich in 1938/39.
Dark grey - Sudetenland, the area of native speaking Germans within the
Czechoslovakian border.
Striped grey - Czechoslovakia.
Gleiwitz is situated just above the furthest point east of the Sudetenland shaded area,
close to the Polish border.
Map credit: Carl Opitz, Geographishe Anshalt.Leipzig 027.

During WW2, young men, and eventually young women, had to work for six months in military style work camps to support the war effort and reduce unemployment figures. These work camps were known as Reichs Arbeits Dienst (RAD). Ursula went to RAD Roeggenfelde (2) Kreis Geogau in April 1943. Christa-Maria went to Wahrenbrück, Kreis Liebenwerda on 14th November 1944, two weeks before her eighteenth birthday.

Chapter Two

Ursula begins her diary

In the Sixth Year of the War, 1945

Diary entries may undoubtedly have distinct reasons for their origin....... But what they have in common is they 'should be a memory' and a reminder, even years later, for both the writer and for our dear fellow human beings, who want to tell of their experiences in this way.

I want to begin with a summary of my life up to now, which will be the background for the actual events; the ones that 'should be a memory.'

Gleiwitz, Easter Sunday 12th April 1925

The happy birth of a healthy little daughter, Ursula Dorothea, welcomed with boundless joy and gratitude by Artur Ciba and his wife, Margarete, née Jurettko.

So, my birthday fell on Easter Sunday, 12th April 1925.

After nineteen months, my dear sister, Christa-Maria Agnes, was born on 29th November 1926. I spent blissful, joyful childhood days with her.

In April 1931, I started school at the Volksschüle 9. After four years there, I was transferred to the high school, and I continued my education until April 1943.

My high school days were interrupted in 1938 by the compulsory change from my private convent school (The Marien Convent School) to a state, yes, purely secular high school - The Eichendorff Oberschüle. Of course, the farewell from the school where Christa-Maria and I had made our First Holy Communion in 1935, was difficult.

Time itself had to heal this pain of separation, although we could still go to the convent chapel for Sunday services and 'Queen of Peace' devotions. The faith teachings with Curate Schenk brought the teachers and my classmates from Class 5 at the Marien Convent School together once again.

I finished my schooling after taking my Abitur (*A levels*) examinations in 1943.

Called up to attend Air Ammunitions Institute in Krappitz!

(*Krappitz is a town in Germany, 60km northwest of Gleiwitz.*)

Means another interruption to my High School, if only for a brief time. My deployment here was during the last 'big holiday' in the summer of 1942. I was torn away from my peaceful life, which I completely enjoyed, to go to the Air Ammunitions factory. I really learned to appreciate the comfort of my parents' home and being able to attend high school to learn and be educated.

Ursula's Class photo, 1943. Eichendorff Oberschüle, Gleiwitz - some of Ursula's friends mentioned in her diary.
Back Row - Right to Left, Ursula Ciba, Uschi Przemeck.
First Middle Row on Right - Ursula Jendralski, then 3rd from left, Liesel Ulbrich.
5th from Left - Teaching Assistant, Alice Pifko.
Front Row - 4th from Left, Hannelore Loske.

April 1943 - January 1945

Shortly after my final school examinations, I was called up for the Reichs Arbeits Dienst (RAD) work camp in Roeggenfelde (2) in the Geogau region. Now it was time to say goodbye to my parents, Christel[3] and my relatives, maybe for a long time? So, on 6th April 1943, I started a new community life, initially with joy towards people at the work camp. My sad farewell mood soon turned into extreme joy when I was told, during the camp examination, that my state of health was not up to RAD demands and I, after two and a half days, envied by almost all the working maids, could go home. Of course, my return so quickly, triggered a great deal of enthusiasm at home. It should be understandable how happy and grateful I was about being sent home, after getting to know 'camp life' in

---

3 Christa-Maria is variously referred to as Christel, Christele or Kitta throughout these diaries.

Krappitz the previous year. Now a time began for me in which I could fully pursue my 'own interests', which often had to take a back seat during school.

Truly, a wonderful time. In August of the same year, I was called up to do Student Compulsory Service - since I didn't complete my six months in RAD - which I did at a Public Welfare institution. The work in this office was extensive and varied. The group of people I worked with was a special one, if only because of their peculiar work. Youth Aid!! I first got to know how bad it is for some people here, from the many cases I have worked on. But rather than that, I will gladly remember the times we had nice get-togethers at the birthday parties in the youth welfare family. After the temporary end of the Student Compulsory Service, I was to be put back into a completely new, but not happy environment. 'Learning, for a life's work', but different than at school, it was now called.

At the end of April 1944, I began my studies at Friedrich Wilhelm University in Breslau. For this first semester, that unfortunately would also be the last for a long time, I was studying Chemistry, Botany, Zoology, Physics and Geography.

I shared a small room with a colleague in a side wing of the honourable Ursuline Convent in the centre of Breslau, Upper Silesia. An enjoyable time for me, during which I just didn't fully use the wonderful freedom, always thinking about the difficult chemistry exam at the beginning of the second semester.

After only a few months at the University in Breslau, suddenly, everything was different; the lecture halls were changed to office space and the laboratories to iron industry workshops.

Steel und Presswork, Gleiwitz - that was my new place of work for a long time. Here I learned a lot about payroll accounting that I had never known before. After this time, on getting orders from 'higher command' I was not able to start my studies again - what to do now?

In December 1944, an application to the military district doctor in Breslau for a position in the laboratory in one of the Gleiwitz-Hindenburg military hospitals was successful. The date of entry into the Gleiwitz-Kaltbad Hospital School was set for 15th Jan 1945. Up to this point, I had planned to take the opportunity to visit my sister at her work camp (RAD) in Wahrenbrück, where she had been since 14th November 1944. If the leadership hadn't been so stubborn about a start date, I could have gone. What a pity, as I was looking forward to seeing Christel again - maybe it wasn't supposed to be?

Shortly before starting work, I was asked to report to the head office for an introduction to the Chief Medical Officer, Doctor Ulbrich and for the recording of exact personal details. The Chief of Staff carried out this 'authentication' with the chief medical officer. After that, an invitation to a nice get-together followed, one can say, as the prelude to the start of duty.

CHAPTER THREE

Christa-Maria leaves her home in Gleiwitz

November 14th 1944

Now it is my turn to work for six months at the RAD camp in Wahrenbrück.

I am sad to leave my family in such uncertain times. One must do one's duty and help the war effort in whatever way one can.

I travel alone by train, reflecting as I look through the window at the passing countryside.

On the way there, behind the fences, bloomed a world of its own; the Heavens placed them here on earth.

At the fences, the poppies had been blooming and over there, the corn had ripened in the field. People have lost and found many things.

One heart is opened, another is broken in two; but corn and red poppies make no cry.

Wahrenbrück, in the Liebenwerda region, an isolated location in the middle of nowhere. About sixty girls, like me, from all over Germany, housed in prefabricated dormitories, to work either on farm or in factory, 7km away. I am to work in the factory making bomb casings. Started work at once on 15th November 1944; woken at 05.30hrs, dressed in brown calico uniform and headscarf. Morning rollcall. A new regimented life for me - extremely arduous work and I know no-one.

The sun's morning rays wake all creatures at dawn. The joyful birds' early chorus greets the light trails. It sings and rejoices everywhere; the forest and meadow awake.

December 12th 1944
Almost a month here and no time to write.

Erika Dollinger, from my school, is here. We are in the same dormitory block and walk the 7km to the factory together, after breakfast in the canteen. Our steamy breath floats away from our faces and each step crunches on the crisp, early morning snow underfoot. It is so cold, by the time we get there, our eyebrows and any wisps of hair not under our scarves, are frozen. Sanding and shaping the wooden casing for V2 bombs all day is dusty and hard on our hands, especially in the cold.

In the evening, simple food is served for everyone. The clatter of cutlery on plates and chatter echoes around the sparse canteen. We eat at long wooden tables, hungry after an exhausting day and long walk to and from the factory. Then we sing patriotic songs, receive instruction from our camp leader or listen to the radio before going to bed.

'Always keep watch, dear comrades, because the enemy is cunning and ready to harm us badly. We always need to be on guard, comrades be ready.'

Good night, my comrades, save this day. The stars move up from the fir trees into the deep blue canopy and sparkle on the world, to banish the darkness. Good night, comrades, keep a strong heart and joy in your eyes, so the day comes happily like a chime, and you are good and ready for it.

10th January 1945, Wahrenbrück.

Dearest Sisterlein,

Many thanks for your letter of 6th January 1945. Since Thursday, we haven't had any work in the factory. On 15th Jan 1945 we must go back there. Two free days didn't feel like any free time at all!

I'm writing this letter in bed, in the evening. Yesterday, I was in the kitchen all day. I wanted to eat my weight in food but didn't have a minute. Today, I was with the bombed-out family from Berlin, who live here in the camp. A medical officer's wife with five children; all cheeky brats, I can tell you. I had to take out the potties and the smallest one had diarrhoea, so I had to empty that during the day as well!

I had to shower four children in the evening. I was eventually finished with this irrepressible pack of brats! The family gets food from the camp. The woman doesn't do any washing up. She also notes down her washing in our laundry books! That's a lady who walks round in her dressing gown all day, lies down in the afternoon, reads and does schoolwork with the two schoolchildren.

Tomorrow, we can sleep in until 10.00hrs

I am directly jealous of the things Wolfhart[4] has sent you. Will the package, which you say is still on the way, be for me? I'm still thinking about how happy we were last year with his surprises.

Oma (*Ciba*) sent me a package with Pfefferkuchen and a small bag of cubed sugar. Your package from 19th December isn't here yet, Uschi.

What did you put in that Christmas cracker for me? What is that little packet? It feels quite hard, and I can't work it out at all! But great, great that I still have something of it to come.

I'll answer the questionnaire another time - I don't have much time today.

I wrote to Wolfhart for Christmas. Maka is not far from me in Cottbus. He writes to me from the hospital that he has a cracked rib. His mother spent the festive days with him.

---

4 Wolfhart is Ursula's beau. Absent from her life since 1943, he is mentioned at various times throughout her diary.

So, you also opened Wistubas' letter? Well, he is a funny penguin!

No-one has found anything out about Vater's letter to the leader - it's a hopeless case. The camp leader isn't here again this week. She is twenty-five years old, big and strong, with a deep voice, unmarried.

By the way, I urgently need the four rubber things, already finished, for me to put on my suspenders.

Uschi, didn't you once make such a good marzipan that you sent me for my last birthday in the blue biscuit tin?

I mean, that would go down very well here.

Is your cold better now?

What is Gabriel doing around town? Isn't she in RAD? What was that about handing things in to the German People's Army (Volkssturm)?

There is a Hannelore Madaus here. Her father, who died two years ago, was the notorious Dr. Madaus from Oucas. Dr. Madaus[5] propagated D8, D12 and so on.

I've gained 1kg. There is a work maid here who weighs 79kg. I now weigh 52kg

I apologise for the scrawl.

Be a thousand times hugged and kissed,

From your Kitta.

P. S Thank you very much for the good Christmas cracker. Say hello to the parents. Sometimes things are all right here but knowing it could go on for such a long time is unbearable. If you really want to know, my nose is truly full up to the brim! (*I'm fed up to the back teeth.*)

Bye.

I didn't have time to read the letter through again.

---

5 Dr. Gerhard Madaus was famous in 1940s Germany for his production of herbal medicines. He developed D8, used for its sedative and calming effects, containing valerian root, passionflower and hop. D12 was used as a digestive aid for indigestion, bloating and cramps containing chamomile peppermint and caraway. His eponymous company became a leading pharmaceutical manufacturer and is still operational today.
Ursula was keen on herbal remedies and would have been interested to know his daughter was at RAD camp with Christa-Maria.

Wahrenbrück, 14th January 1945

Vater's 50th birthday.

Today, on Vater's 50th birthday, I'm naturally thinking a lot of you and our home. This first letter I am writing is for you. Even if I don't have a letter to answer, or much to say, I want to at least talk to you by letter.

So, so sad that I cannot be with you all at home today. I think to myself of Mutti's 50th birthday. It is a nice coincidence that your 50th birthdays both fell on a Sunday; so even though I am not there, I can imagine your day of celebrations.

No-one has said anything about Vater's letter to the work camp leader. I was recently asked for my home address by the camp administration; I didn't think anything of this question until the evening, when, reading a letter from you, written by Vater, a light went on. Have you already received a letter from the staff here at Wahrenbrück?

Early this morning, I went with three other work maids to Liebenwerda to attend Mass. It wasn't too cold, but it was icy, and once I slipped and sat down hard on my bottom! I went early to the other dormitory to wake two other girls who wanted to come with me and Eva Meissner. It's always quite embarrassing when everyone else wakes up too! Then you must go to the work leader and sign out and off duty - so you must cheer them up too because you're going out. So far everyone has been well-behaved.

In future, we will have to get up even earlier on Sundays because they are changing the Mass times from 07.45hrs to 07.00hrs since the men must go to the People's Army (Volkssturm) and would otherwise be too late. We'll have to set off at 06.00hrs.

I was so happy to have a proper Sunday - the long road ahead doesn't seem so endless!

I was very tired in the morning, but I had planned to go to church for Vater's birthday. Then I prayed a lot for my people in the church and to God - may his Kingdom come to them.

These folk don't let themselves get sucked in and believe that their way is the only right way to do things. It hurts me so much when I see they would rather make a pilgrimage to the cinema in Liebenwerda on a Sunday afternoon, without any thought of sending praise and thanks to heaven on the Lord's Day.

You wouldn't believe how difficult it is to make sure the Lord is also faithfully served by others. Then they speak grandly about how good a Catholic they are.

The preparations for Christmas celebrations, among people from the former Poland, seemed to consist only of not eating meat for three days before the festival. Here, they 'keep' this custom in such a way, that on the Thursday before Christmas Eve, (Sunday) they buy themselves 800g of sausage! Oh, one could cry when one sees all this and how little one's beliefs are understood. I imagined it to be easier. Or I trusted myself too much.

Now, apart from Monday, I haven't been in the factory for the whole of last week. I was in the kitchen, and I liked working there, despite it being lots of demanding work. While the people from the farm and housekeeping finish their work at 17.30hrs, the kitchen staff can't finish work until after dinner. I have noticed there is much better food at lunchtime, when there are fewer people, than in the evening when everyone is there. On Tuesday, we had pea soup (from dried peas) with potato dumplings and for afters there was 'poor man's' Ritter (chocolate substitute). Unfortunately, there was only one Ritter left for the four of us working in the kitchen.

On Wednesday, working with the family from Berlin, we had jacket potato and gravy with undercooked, breaded, fried turnip slices.

On Thursday we were allowed to sleep until 10 am - cabbage wraps for lunch.

Friday lunch was semolina soup, fried potatoes and red cabbage.

Saturday lunch, potato soup, that I made almost completely by myself! I stirred it for a long time, so it didn't stick and burn at the bottom. We baked cakes - licked the spoons and tasted the mixture. For pudding we had a piece of fresh, sweet, cake; for the kitchen there is of course a little more. I also ate my fill of the burnt bits, from the tins, with sugar.

Yesterday, I had my picture taken, standing at the hot oven behind steaming pots, while stirring with a wooden spoon. Hopefully, something will come of it. In the afternoon, I sliced fifteen wholegrain loaves by hand using a saw knife like the one we have at home. The bread machine was not needed - and anyway, it only cuts thick 'buzzes' (that's how they say 'slices' here.)

I hid myself a slice and, in the evening, toasted it and had it with butter! When I ate the toast that was so crispy, I always think to myself of the quality crispbreads (knekkerbrot) that we ate in Breslau, Uschi. There, you really entertained me well!

Ah, where are all these nice times now?

After lunch - (using a different pen) I prefer writing with the other pen, but my hands look as though I wrote the first part with dipping ink!

Today we had rouladen,[6] cauliflower and peeled potatoes for lunch. For dessert, semolina pudding decorated with jam and roasted oat flakes.

Then a thought came to me - these great oat flakes, one could make oneself in the kitchen oven. One has a small such tin; perhaps they could occasionally give me some oat flakes and sugar. Butter I could also buy here. One gets so spoiled here; you wouldn't believe it!

I've completely lost my blisters here. Even the woollen socks don't bother me anymore.

Today the air-raid alarm went - we see the bombs being dropped on Dresden, but we didn't feel anything and didn't bother about it any further. Only the flag was lowered. Now, we only see the flag on Sunday. By the way, this is in the service of our camp leader. In the week, there was nothing to do with the armaments. We don't need to do any morning exercise either. In the mornings at 05.30hrs, the camp leader comes to the dormitory and says, "Good Morning - Everyone up!" After ten minutes she appears again to inspect our lockers - our clothes to be folded neatly to specific measurements, our wooden stools and wash bowls scrubbed clean, repeatedly until the leader is satisfied. In addition, we must stand in our cloaks, and the bedcovers should already be turned back precisely. Curlers should no longer be dangling in our hair. After, breakfast we line up in front of the camp leader's house. A woman from the war office dismisses all the female armament workers and will report back with further instructions in the evening.

---

6 Traditionally, rouladen is made from thinly sliced and pounded beef, rolled up with a filling of onions, bacon and pickles, secured with string and braised in a rich gravy. During the war, these ingredients were scarce, so one can assume, in the work camp, substitutes were used, or ingredients omitted altogether.

(*Written along the edge of the page* - Today the crib was tidied away from the church in Liebenwerda)

On Friday, I must go shopping. In the morning I cycle to Wildgrübe, 5km away, get 2kg of pork for the evening casserole. I'm sure you've never ridden through a scary forest on a bike before. I've done it twice! On the way back it was a bit better, although I had to carry nineteen small bricks that I found in the forest, in the basket on the crossbar, in addition to the meat. A porter, for this serious method of transport, I had not! After lunch I had to go again to Liebenwerda, on the bicycle. I went there with an empty bucket. But from Liebenwerda, I don't know how I got back to the camp house. On one side of the crossbar, a full bucket of quark, *(cream cheese)* the other side, nets with butter and margarine. With the ice and snow the bicycle slid about all over the place. Mutti, I can tell you, I almost didn't arrive in one piece!

What are you doing right now, I wonder? Perhaps you've had a fine drink of wine for the celebration today. The only drink here is black coffee. Today, for once, we had white coffee. Yesterday, Saturday, I had my last piece from the cracker you sent at Christmas. It certainly lasted well because I was working in the kitchen for four days. Did you go to mass at 08.00hrs? At 08.00hrs, I was also in church just now. Was Oma there again? What did you have for the celebratory roast? What kind of meal is being arranged for Monday evening? Perhaps I will also get a piece of cake - surely Mutti has done some baking!

Now I don't know what more to write about.

Be all heartily greeted and kissed,

From Your,

Christel

Now only two and a half months RAD time left.

Chapter Four

The Russian Invasion of Gleiwitz

12ᵗʰ January 1945, Gleiwitz

Oma Ciba's birthday.

My Grandmother celebrated her 73ʳᵈ birthday with us. At the same time, this day sees the beginning of the Great Eastern Offensive.

News item, 13ᵗʰ January 1945 - the first believable bulletin came on Sunday evening 'Rapid Advance of Soviets towards Vistula River.' [7]

14ᵗʰ January 1945

Vater's 50ᵗʰ birthday. On this day of honour, let Curate Schenk say a holy mass for us, probably the most precious gift, in these circumstances.

15ᵗʰ January 1945

Starting work in the Kaltbad Hospital School. In the evening of the same day, a nice get-together for Vater's birthday party with Onkel Joseph, Tante Liesel and Rosel. Coming home from the laboratory, I quickly

---

7 The Vistula River runs almost south/north through Poland and comes within 100km of Gleiwitz, to the west.

helped Mutti, as one does on these family occasions, with table decorations and preparing a splendid dinner. I approached such work, where one can let the imagination run wild and show one's style, with a special love. Who would have believed that this evening, sitting round the table together, was to be the last of many happy hours spent with my family at home.

Christel's absence from the 50th birthday party, naturally, made us a little sad. How nice it was, every previous year, when she was part of the celebrations. What might she be doing now, while we are sitting comfortably together?

On this question, I haven't had an answer from you, Christel. I can hardly believe it! Your letter of 10th January 1945 - which I received at home today, 15th January 1945, was the last sign of life from you.

The terrible war cast a dark shadow over the conviviality of the evening, and on our immediate future. We went along with what was politically prepared and inevitably being rolled forward, but in this moment, we didn't want it and couldn't accept it as a certain fate for us, still hoping for a happy turnaround from this critical situation.

16th January 1945
Work in the laboratory. In the evening, our last seminar with Curate Schenk, interrupted by air-raid sirens at 21.20hrs.

17th January 1945

Everywhere on the main thoroughfares, there are prisoners[8], under armed guard, marching to the West. Air-raid sirens sound and flare bombs dropped!

18th January 1945

Extremely cold - 35 degrees below zero.

Laboratory work at the military hospital to be suspended. Air-raid sirens all day.

Late in the afternoon the following message comes through: 'Gleiwitz to be evacuated in 24 hours!' In the following hours, High Command issues so many different, conflicting orders!

One could go completely insane!

19th January 1945

Retreating soldiers command the streets. Air-raid sirens all day long. Parcels from Tante Dorchen arrived. One, made up for Christel, will no longer be accepted by the post office. My poor little bird, our Pips, who gave us so much joy with his whistle and trusting behaviour, died this afternoon. I no longer felt any real sadness about it - I could only envy the green feathered little fellow his rest, when thinking of the grizzly future that awaits us.

20th January 1945

Warwas and Hübner families leave Gleiwitz and we are alone in the apartment building. In the afternoon, at 12.20hrs Vater received a phone

---

8 Refers to prisoners on The Death March

call to say that hospital laboratory would be temporarily moved to Ober Schreiberhau at 14.00hrs today. I can't make up my mind to go. I feel afraid. Vater gets angry about this behaviour and keeps going on at me for so long that I can't stand his reproaches any longer.

I am forced to quickly get 'travel ready.' So, I find myself, with accompanying parents, at the Wehrmacht train station. Here, the people are crushed together like grapes, everyone trying, with all their might, pushing and shoving, to escape the terror by fleeing. The trains are full-people climb on the roofs and cling to doors and bumpers with one hand, the other one clutching their belongings. Families try to keep together; parents reach for outstretched arms and search for fingertips as children are separated in the crush and sway of the crowd. Such a noise! Sirens! Screaming! Crying and calling out for those separated from a family group. The smell of oil and smoke, the hiss of steam. Terrible fear and overwhelming homesickness come upon me while waiting for the train. I beg Mutti incessantly to take me home again. I just cannot bear to leave home, knowing my parents will stay behind. Vater was not allowed to leave the office and Mutti didn't want to leave without him. In short, they had no plans to come back to the station the next day or day after that. The knowledge of Mutti being left behind made me so torn inside that I had to use every strength and determination to be allowed to go home again.

This constant struggle made me extremely sick and weary. Vater forced me to leave, with all his might and stubbornly persisted with his demands.

Mutti, who tried to persuade me, in her kind way, that it was right to leave, took pity on me in my torment and helped me say "I want to go home again" to Vater, which was not easy.

Feeling a little better and saved from terrible distress, I found myself panicking again, when entering the station forecourt, packed with jostling and shrieking people, from where we could go home. Even if it were only a matter of days that we could live as free people, I was extremely grateful that this fight with Vater had ended like this. Just the thought, yes, the awareness of not being alone, made everything easier for me to endure what was forthcoming and destined for the near future.

21.00hrs air-raid sirens and bombing on the tram tracks by Skobel Brewery.

21st January 1945

At 08.00hrs, feeling much stronger and calmer than the day before, I go to Sunday Mass in the chapel of the convent school. Here, I met various friends, each dealing with the coming events of the next few days. From Liesel Ulbrich, a classmate, I learn all sorts of important things about the advancing Russian fronts. Her brother has been employed as a reporting driver in a unit stationed at our barracks in Gleiwitz since yesterday.

Onkel Josef and Frau Hüttner visit us during the day. In the evening we pay a short visit to the Kubele family. Our glasses filled with red wine, there is a pleasant atmosphere, at least on the surface, while we strive to cope with the war events that are still part of the future. Wishing each other good luck, we part. On the way home we encounter soldiers with prisoners walking slowly towards the West.

22nd January 1945

During the day, endless air-raid sirens! Thousands of prisoners of war pass by us, heading for the West. Late in the afternoon, Mutti and I go to town; but before that, I must go to fetch Vater from his work. However, we did not meet one another because his office had received a proclamation from the Deputy District Manager. All companies to continue working and to defend their homeland. While these slogans are broadcast through the airwaves, local police are ordering businesses to close at once. Around 18.00hrs there is heavy artillery fire from the direction of Laband[9]; the war is now rumoured to be in our immediate vicinity, so that we expect our hometown to be occupied this very night.

23rd January 1945

The code name 'Crane' should be given for the evacuation of those who remained in the town until now. The code word doesn't come through. Everything is haywire. The main roads are blocked with soldiers, refugees, laden carts and cars.

When Vater comes home from the office mid-morning, there is no way for us to get ahead. He has been told by returning fellow citizens that it is 'murder' to go out on the roads now, so we gave up the intention of fleeing almost completely. I still had a little hope of escaping reasonably quickly and safely. Out of this hope, I ventured between 13.00 - 14.00hrs, to the Keith Barracks to find Liesel Ulbrich. Barely through the guard station when heavy fire started from the Laband[10] forest meadow, so I had to find an air-raid shelter. After some time, with bullets cracking and bursting over us, it was quiet once more. A soldier led me at once to Liesel Ulbrich's dormitory. I don't hear anything specific from her either; they are also still unclear about their time of departure. With good wishes, we

9 Police and military were known to give different orders. Laband is a town 7km north of Gleiwitz on the east side of the Klodnitz river which runs through Gleiwitz.
10 Laband was occupied by Russian forces on 24th January 1945 and came under Polish administration. The Russian Ministry of Internal Affairs set up internment camps for German and Polish-speaking Silesians. Several thousand people were held there and deported to the Soviet Union for forced labour.

say goodbye to each other. I then go home, running and accompanied by the occasional thunder of artillery fire.

The air-raid shelter is being prepared by the parents, the laundry room oven is moved and reassembled in the cellar corridor, where only we could stay. I pray that Christel will go west with other comrades. We crawl into the basement as the shelling continues. At night we venture upstairs to our beds, where we spend the night fully clothed, praying, amid heavy shooting. It is horrible, how the stillness of the icy January night is being torn apart by the repeated thunder of heavy artillery fire.

23rd January 1945. 10.00hrs, Gleiwitz.

My dear Christa,

Quickly today, a few lines for you, which I hope will reach you via the town of Oppeln.

We haven't heard anything from you since Thursday, 18th January 1945. It's a shame that we couldn't get the parcel from Tante Dorchen off to you as well.

I want to ask the post office today, if registered mail is accepted, then we can open the parcel and divide it into two and send as two smaller ones. Except for a 'very nice' shootout yesterday, everything is going on as usual here.

What is happening here on Raudener Strasse, the columns of soldiers and people from the east going further west, is indescribable. We always thought we saw a lot here in September 1939 but everything happening now in this moment, surpasses that several times over. Hübner and Warwas families left with their children on Saturday evening. There are still so many of our friends out there, where are they all going? Rosel went home to Frau Kahlert. So, don't you worry at all, dear little Kitta; Gleiwitz was saved so wonderfully before - why not again this time?

All the best.

Many greetings and kisses to you.

From Vater, Mutti and me

24th January 1945

Around o8.oohrs soldiers and OT men,[11] sparsely armed it seemed to me, came from the barracks into the city, where terrible things were bound to happen. Plumes of smoke were already rising to heaven at this time. We tried to find out what had fallen victim to the flames. Repeatedly, German assault rifles thundered past, we couldn't even agree if they were directly involved in the fight. Around midday, Vater and I ventured back towards the city when some OT men backed away. They had fought hard on Peter Paul Square. It would have been crazy to go there; the Russian enemy are rolling in with tremendous force, from all sides - with murderous shrieks and hissing whistles from the infantry shelling. It is high time to seek out the cellar again - the little ceasefire was over. That night, the three of us can no longer stand it in the cold cellar corridor. So, we sneak quietly through the desolate house and stay upstairs. This night too is spent like the previous one. Praying, we await the next morning, not knowing if we will see it.

25th January 1945

Heavy fighting in Gleiwitz city centre. Large fires cover the city in front of us, (Kloster Strasse - The Ring - Mansfield Strasse) Screeching bullets, impact after impact crashes and thunders; the infantry shelling hisses and whistles above us, crashing onto the wrecked houses and pavements at close range. While we are holding out in the basement, the light and water supply are cut off! After midnight the roar of battle subsided significantly, the last heavy shots had been fired. Up to this point in time we had not yet seen a 'victorious soldier.'

---

11 OT stands for Organisation Todt, a civil and military engineering organisation in Germany from 1933 - 1945, named after its founder, Fritz Todt, who was an engineer and senior Nazi. Notorious for using forced labour from 1943 - 1945, OT oversaw all construction of concentration camps, to supply forced labour to German industries.

26ᵗʰ January 1945

Our brave warriors must retreat to the West; so, the battle in Gleiwitz ends! Around 17.oohrs the first Russian soldiers pass by us. In their earth brown, shabby uniforms, they roll their tanks through the snow-covered streets, still heavily armed, towards the outskirts of the town behind us. They shoot in windows of ruined houses - several bullet holes made just below our dining room and kitchen window, then directly at Hübner and Warwas', many more shots in their dining room and study windows. Did you think that you would find some remaining pockets of resistance and flush them out, with no mercy? In the cellars of the houses still lived in, at 7 Lüdendorff Strasse,[12] we waited anxiously for the first encounter with the 'victors'. What was going on inside of me in these moments, I cannot put into words. The tremendous fear, dread and uncertainty that plagues me to the point of exhaustion makes me, and all those suffering with me, jump and startle at the slightest noise. Only those who have experienced such hours with their crushing effect, sometimes re-lived much later, can understand or empathise with me.

We sneak, thank God, not into the basement where those beasts are looking to make 'home', but into our flat. We are shocked to see where the fire has spread; the city centre is a sea of flames drawing in.

27ᵗʰ January 1945

A bit of silence sets in. We see individual Russian soldiers passing by. Today, we hear the first news bulletin about the battle.

---

12 The Ciba family lived at 5, Paul Keller Strasse. Paul Keller (1873 - 1932) was a writer and journalist known for his socialist and pacifist views and a vocal opponent of German militarism and imperialism. The street was renamed Lüdendorff Strasse in 1933 after Erich Lüdendorff, a German general and military strategist. This was part of a wider initiative by the Nazi regime to remove the names of Jewish and socialist figures from public spaces.

28th January 1945

The last days of the past week have taken a lot out of me, so I must lie down. Mutti dares to go to Mass in a private house on Raudener Strasse. I pray at home, the prayers of today's Sunday Mass. In general, there is calm and further news bulletin about the battle. Even today, high blazing flames illuminate the evening sky.

29th January 1945

Russian soldiers pushed their way to the Gleiwitz barracks with all their entourage and occupied the area west of Gleiwitz. At night, we are threatened by dagger wielding, drunk Russian soldiers who have come into our apartment building. We had to give them two watches. It happened in breathtaking seconds; how I jumped out of bed with Mutti, while Vater opened the house door to this madman banging wildly at the front door with the dagger. My limbs tremble with fear and rage, that I can't put my slippers on quickly enough or put on any other clothes. I stand there in my pyjamas and winter coat, as this rumbling and screaming beast in the form of a man, gets ever closer to our flat. Luckily, apart from the loss of the watches mentioned above, this 'visitor' passed somewhat unpleasantly by us.

30th January 1945

Fairly quiet during the day after this incident. Have decided to sleep at Herr Wegmann's tonight at the Long Row, where it feels safer to be in a row of joined houses. At around 16.30hrs we trudge to the back of the cellar, through a knee-deep, snow-covered yard, and arrive at Herr Wegmann's with a little hand luggage. After praying the rosary together, we went into a new bed. I slept with my Mutti but couldn't fall asleep at all, always thinking of last night's robbery and predicting the terrible things that would happen this night too. Mutti, however, takes me away from these thoughts; maybe because she simply couldn't believe them and didn't want them in her mind anymore.

31st January 1945

Coming back from Herr Wegmann's in the morning with anxious beating hearts to see if our house has been engulfed in flames last night. As we approach, we can tell the opposite and look confidently towards our apartment on the second floor at 5, Ludendorff Strasse. Standing in front of the door to the building, we see not everything had gone well. My hunches from the night before hadn't cheated me! It looked awful, like an earthquake that had trembled and subsided. The front door and all the doors to the apartments were smashed in; our apartment looked devastating; most of what we had was looted. We couldn't tell what was missing in the tangled mess. The piano had been taken apart; the desk had been broken open with force and everything in the cupboards and drawers had been strewn all over the floor. The kitchen, pantry and cellar had remained untouched until then. During the day, we stay in this mess yet were not bothered by Russians again, despite the open front door. But in the face of such danger, that could arise from not being able to close the door, we go back to Herr Wegmann's in the late afternoon, to 'sleep'. I go to bed with the same anxious feeling. It is Mutti who calms me with her observation,

"Well, if they see such a destroyed apartment, they won't go in any further." Comforting words .... But .... It could be completely different, and I could be completely right again because ....

CHAPTER FIVE

Ursula's life under Russian Occupation

1st February 1945

In the morning we are no longer allowed in our home because the Russians live there - now Russian quarter. Ten men end up with Family Lamla at 20, Katzler Strasse, in their first-floor apartment. In the afternoon, we are eyewitnesses to this as we carry out our suitcases. We stand at Lamla's window, as if rooted there, looking at the appalling goings on, but unable to fight back or defend ourselves. Since the Loske's are sleeping at Lamla's with Fräulein Grziwotch, who were all burned out, we go to Zimmerman's abandoned apartment at 20, Katzler Strasse, on the second floor.

2nd February 1945

Maria Candlemas, Sacred Heart Friday, church attendance at the Kreutzkirche. Today, the parents are allowed into the apartment. I stay at Lamla's. Vater's last suitcase with jewellery and gold, savings bank books and medicines are stolen from Zimmerman's apartment, including my leather pencil case with Pelikan fountain pen. I was able to save the backpack with some groceries and jewellery.

3rd February 1945

Drunken Russians romp around the Warwas' and Hübner's flats. The parents sleep again today at our home, otherwise the apartment would be confiscated from us as 'uninhabited'. I find a place to sleep at Arndt's, next to Lamla's in 20, Katzler Strasse. At night, there are terrible detonations because German bombs attack the Russian supply lines (Plesser & Nicholas Strasse). Stay at Lamla's during the day. Went at noon with Mutti to see the Hrübasik family and to the school monastery. Artillery fire at close range.

I sleep at Lamla's on the dining room floor.

4th February 1945

Day of the Lord! Going to mass at All Saints' Church. Then I dare to go to the school monastery where I meet Uschi Przemeck - she is left behind and all alone.

A somewhat more restful day. Again, I sleep at Lamla's.

5th February 1945

Russian soldiers are still in our home and take all the supplies out of the basement, including our bikes on which they 'learn to ride'. Parents are allowed into the basement with guard escort.

6th February 1945

Still the plundering and robbing continues - they willingly take what the earlier looters left behind.

7th February 1945

As difficult as it is for us, we have to part with our beautiful Telefunken radio. I go with Mutti to the delivery point, in front of the museum on Niederwall Strasse. A Russian official and an interpreter, stop us: "It's a good radio and it plays well?" They liked it, naturally, and it was taken from us in return for a receipt written in Russian. (An unfriendly exchange of words with the interpreter, who is angry that we are not Russian speaking Germans!) Then we come across Frau Kachel, who leads us in front of her burnt-out house and tearfully tells us that her husband has been shot.

8th February 1945

Russian soldiers are leaving our house with bags of riches - we have become poor! Our parents find some of our things in the devastated cellar, although Christel's suitcase has already been looted.

9th February 1945

Vater starts to fix the house front door and the door to our apartment. Luckily, it works - until now, everything was open. Now, at least, we can lock the doors again.

10th February 1945

In the morning, I go to our apartment to try and tidy up the terrible mess that is there. Plundering Commander and his Captain come into our apartment again. Spent the night at the Warwas' house and took everything that was left, there: beds, carpets, curtains, mattresses, even left-over pewter jars from our cellar. Sleep at Lamla's.

At around 19.00hrs, two Russian officers come into our apartment, talk to the parents and then demand they gather their stuff together and leave.

11th February 1945

Day of the Lord - Go to church at Kreuzkirche. On the way there, looting of the surviving dwellings, a terrible picture of devastation, presents itself to us. The curtains were torn from the windows in a rough and disturbing way, cupboards cleaned out, carpets pulled up, and everything thrown through the windows onto the carts. Even the grandfather clock has been robbed from our house today! This evening, the two Russian officers from yesterday, are upstairs again and want to see if our stuff has already been cleared away. They wander round our home, touching and looking at what is left. They look at photographs and try to find Christa and me in the photograph hanging in the dining room. They couldn't find us that quickly.

12th February 1945

During the day, I was again at our apartment to tidy up the mess. I am slowly finding my way out of this confusion, but for the most part, I have taken it badly. Otherwise, relatively quiet.

13th February 1945

Go with Mutti to Onkel Joseph; there we get some laundry soap and other useful things. Then clean up in our apartment again. Three officers come in the afternoon looking for quarters. I hide and it eventually ends well when they leave. Since today the water supply has started again, we no longer need to spend many hours going backwards and forwards to the frozen water pump on Röntgengasse, hooded and disguised like old women, since water carriers were particularly coveted, often looted, goods.

14th February 1945

At Warwas' apartment - Vater finds his stamp album, your Mason jars, Mutti, and tinned vegetables stuffed under some wine bottles. There was immense joy over this.

15th February 1945

Day passed quietly. Went to our apartment again - more tidying up!

16th February 1945

Relatively calm today. After the Russian announcement, all men aged 15 - 45 must report to the area near the front and get ready....... allegedly.

17th February 1945

The day passed pretty much like the day before.

18th February 1945

Day of the Lord. Went to church at the Eichendorff Oberschüle. For a few weeks we have been hearing a sermon again. "Where does this sorrow come from? It comes from murder!"

Afternoon with Mutti to Stations of the Cross at the monastery. Afterwards, we make a short visit to Tante Liesel.

19th February 1945

Went to Onkel Joseph's with Mutti. We're genuinely concerned about the men being brought out and taken for interrogation.

20th February 1945

Relatively peaceful; nevertheless, gangs of robbers still roam the streets and plunder people's homes, taking what they want.

21st February 1945

Holy Communion at home with Fr. Kasper. In the afternoon, eight rabid Russians were in the apartment. So, I had to run across the attic floorboards to another house while the soldiers ravaged our apartment. Luckily, they were chased out, in confusion, by an approaching Russian officer.

22nd February 1945

Tante Liesel came by. Onkel Edi extremely ill again - haemorrhage. Otherwise, quiet.

23rd February 1945

At Steiner's, Russian soldiers smash the balcony door to pieces and climb into their apartment. This gang then came to us, and it was something we had to bear.

24th February 1945

Onkel Joseph and Frau Kachel here - otherwise quiet, except for the uncertainty over the 'round up' of the men.

25th February 1945

Day of the Lord - go to church at the school monastery.

The sermon - What does the sorrow mean for us?

1. Punishment.

2. Warning.

3. Conversion.

Frau Hüttner visits us. Vater is caught by Russians, while going to church, and is sent for work.

26 - 28th February 1945

Relatively quiet days.

CHAPTER SIX

Ursula struggles on in Gleiwitz

1st March 1945

R elatively quiet. Afternoon in the city to visit the Kampe family and Frau Rüst.

The fire barricade on the bridge over the Klodnitz canal has been breached.

2nd March 1945

Relatively calm day. Been to Frank, district manager of the Anti-Fascist Blocks, because we need a shovel.[13]

---

13 The rubble remains of destroyed, bombed-out buildings had to be cleared by Germans, often ex National Socialist Party (NSP) members, using spades, picks and shovels. Because there was no civil administration and the Russian Military were not concerned with tidying the town, 'Reconstruction Action Committees' (RAC), took it upon themselves to organise NSP members to clear the rubble. Even young women, who had been part of the League of German Girls, (Bund Deutscher Mädel - BDM) were required to do penal labour clearing rubble. Those summoned to work, had to comply and bring their own tools, often being rounded up on Sundays and forced to work for several hours at a time. The RAC was really a front for the Anti-Fascist Committee; a coalition of anti-Nazis who wanted to take denazification and reconstruction into their own hands in a non-bureaucratic way.

3rd March 1945

Heavy snow fall, needed to shovel the pavements.

Women from 15 - 45 must go to Old Gleiwitz, Kieferstadtel and Schönwald to strengthen the trenches. A lot of agitation and uncertainty among the Russians.

4th March 1945

Day of the Lord. Church in school monastery - sermon was about suffering as a test, a revelation of the human character. In the afternoon we wanted to visit Tante Liesel, but we couldn't get through the door - she wasn't there!

Where can she be with Onkel Edi and Oma Herbst?

5th March 1945

At 07.00hrs, Mutti takes me to the city hospital which has been moved from Friedrick Strasse to the Catholic orphanage at Teucher Strasse because the building must be cleared. My medical exemption certificate from Dr. Massek should be renewed since I am exempt from all the shovelling. Unfortunately, it is not my turn to see Dr. Angela Klüber today, who had to stay behind, on the Russian Commander's order, for a long time. Mutti came to pick me up at 12.30hrs.

6th March 1945

Relatively quiet. Frank, from upstairs, will take me to the hospital tomorrow.

7th March 1945

Frank didn't come - hospital visit postponed until Friday.

8th March 1945

Tante Liesel came to see us. She must clear her apartment for the Russians and now lives in the back of the shop, (*Miethoff's*) which has burnt down. Vater is assigned to work in the abandoned apartments.

9th March 1945

Have not been to the hospital because now, suddenly, I'm given my old sickness certificate - the women must shovel again every day.

10th March 1945

Women used for shovelling. Military station to be built on Runaberg Strasse. Men lead away under guard - a grisly picture.

11th March 1945

Day of the Lord - Church at Kreutzkirche 10.45hrs. Very cold. Went with Mutti to Tante Liesel in the afternoon (Baier-Villa, at the old transmitter on Raudener Strasse and other buildings in the city, burn.)

12th March 1945

Very unsettled night. Magda Wittich came to visit in the afternoon. Onkel Joseph also visited.

13th March 1945

Hacked the ice off all three balconies because the underlying water was running into our apartment. In the afternoon, went with Mutti to wish Onkel Joseph a Happy Birthday.

14th March 1945

Nothing of note.

15th March 1945

It is Mausi's birthday today. I wonder where she's likely to spend the day.

Relatively quiet until 16.00hrs. Vater is again working in the abandoned apartments and is hardly back when a Russian soldier and civilian from GPU (*Soviet State Political Directorate, Russian Intelligence Service and Secret Police*) arrive at 17.00hrs. I cannot and do not want to go back to this point. What happened in those terrible moments and stirred up our innermost beings, I cannot put into words. We had a small ray of hope in these horrible moments when the Russian soldier, with his declaration that Vater would be brought back by 23.00hrs, was not lying to us in the meanest way. Should we believe these promises? I wait with Mutti the whole night for Vater's return, but ... he doesn't come back.

16th March 1945

The two guys from yesterday evening come into the house with victorious, confident swagger, demanding, on Vater's instructions, Schnapps for the Commandant. What lies they're telling us again! Unfortunately, they do manage to get hold of the Schnapps and we couldn't fight back against them. A short time later, Vater is led past us, under guard! Why??? I still have the chance to pack him a small suitcase with some food and wash things.......

But, to our immense joy, Vater comes home at around 13.00hrs on 16th March 1945.

17th March 1945
The day was quiet.

18th March 1945
Day of the Lord - church at the school monastery. Sermon - hold yourself well in the distress. Onkel Joseph comes in the afternoon, then I go with Mutti to Tante Liesel.

19th March 1945
Polish Militia are to be 'received' into Gleiwitz. The most unbelievable preparations are made. From the window, I see red and white flags have been hung out everywhere around here. Suddenly, the anger rises in me!

20th March 1945
At around 07.00hrs, while I am still in bed, rabid Russian soldiers come and take me, with Frau Lamla, to work; specifically to document the Russian graves in Prüssenplatz, which has been converted into a cemetery.

21st March 1945
Quiet day. Units of Russian soldiers withdraw.

22nd - 24th March 1945

Relatively quiet days - except for the frightening air operations of the Russians.

25th March 1945

Day of the Lord. Church only at Kreutzkirche.

Fear of leaving our apartment because the Polish are out looking for apartments; but it is going quite well, early this Palm Sunday morning. Mutti has done a lot of work, packing up some things in readiness. In church today, during Mass, it is announced that services may no longer be prayed in German (went to Confession).

26th - 27th March 1945

Relatively quiet days.

28th March 1945

20, Katzler Strasse is to be cleared; therefore, the entire day we schlepp all Lamla and Sollich's things to our's and Hübner's apartments. Today, I finally sleep in our home again.

29th March 1945

20, Katzler Strasse is allowed to go back. We help with rearranging, and I also help with tidying at Lamla's apartment. After that, I sweep the street and the cellar in our apartment building.

30th March 1945

Went to Church with Vater - Good Friday. This time we won't be able to do our Good Friday hike to the Holy Sepulchre, as we have done for many years. It is too restless and dangerous. Vater goes to Reinke once in the morning, working in the garden area. Tante Elly came to visit this afternoon; then we go to bathe, exclusively, at Lamla's.

31st March 1945

Wowitzki takes furniture for himself from Warwas' apartment. Tante Liesel comes to visit; I decorate the little altar at home ready for Easter Day.

CHAPTER SEVEN

A birthday and a move for Ursula

1st April 1945

Easter Sunday. Church in the school monastery. On the way there, we are snatched for work as Berg und Hüttenmann![14] Is this how our Easter Sunday church visit should end? That shouldn't be allowed, and with all due diligence I'm fortunate to find an opportunity to get away with Mutti. We even manage to attend the festive service in the school monastery. That was a special Easter joy for us. We meet Magda Wyrwoll and Fräulein Erdhütter there. At 14:00hrs People Control again!

Vater was again taken by Russians, namely, to the Bismarck Strasse. What I say to myself, as I follow him, hooded and at a distance behind is "Why did something so terrible have to happen to us on this day of resurrection?" I can't believe it!

At about 17.00hrs Uschi Przemeck comes to see me. She stays the night with us. We have a lot to tell each other, until long after midnight, since we are seeing each other for the first time since the occupation.

---

14 Berg und Hüttenmann is a term used to describe a person who works in the mining and metallurgical industries. Jobs included miners, smelters and metal workers. Gleiwitz was a major coal mining centre in Germany and had several iron and steel foundries.

2nd April 1945

Easter Monday. No church today. Vater came back home at 08.00hrs. Fr. Kasper and Onkel Joseph visit us. We have a nice coffee with Uschi - it is white coffee made with skimmed milk powder. I baked a gooseberry and cranberry torte. Mutti and I take Uschi back home to Keith Strasse and then we spent a short visit at the Lamla family.

3rd April 1945

Relatively quiet. I do some darning in the morning. Vater is ordered again to Bismarck Strasse. He should be back by 18.00hrs.

4th - 5th April 1945

Quiet days. Onkel Joseph and Jochen visit us on 4th April.

6th April 1945

Vater went early morning to see the Doctor. Frau Kachel has lunch with us.

Polish housing commissioner visits our apartment at around midday. We fear being seized and thrown out of our home. Tante Liesel comes by later.

7th April 1945

Onkel Joseph visits us again today. Dominik, upstairs, is waiting for Franck, who is at Bismarck Strasse waiting for Vater. Everything went fine there. Latest decision: we are to move to the little Kobyletzki's apartment, who on 25th January, was turfed out of his home, with everything on his bicycle. I am horrified by such a plan, but we can't save ourselves from it.

8th April 1945

The Lord's Day. Went to church at Kreuzkirche. Notifications and sermon in Polish.

Otherwise, quiet. Thoughts of change. Lovely spring weather today. I collect some flowering forsythia branches for Tante Elly's birthday. Visited Lamla's. Terrible vibration at about 21.00hrs??????

9th April 1945

The parents tidy up rooms at Kobyletzki's apartment. Urgent news update - women between 15 - 50 must go to Poland and Russia for three months construction work. How much of this is true, no-one knows officially! Poles let us know we would do well if we went to the German Quarter in Öhringen.(*Öhringen is 850km west of Gleiwitz. The town became a centre for fleeing refugees.*) Tante Elly is fifty years old today. Around 17.30hrs, I go with Mutti to congratulate her. Amazingly, your birthday falls on this day too, dear Hannelore. A little letter should have at least reached you on this day. Unfortunately, I am not allowed to send it in time to reach you. How are you doing? Were you able to celebrate your birthday in peace?

10th April 1945

Beginning of the move, we slept in our apartment even so.

11th April 1945

We were in the middle of moving when we had a surprise visit from the Russians at around midday. Went off reasonably well. In the evening, with Vater, I come straight from Kobyletzki's apartment for supper at our old apartment, when we are attacked by thieving gangs of Russians. I barely have time, just in my work clothes and light straw shoes, to escape! Where to now? Frau Grosse takes me in off the street and I end up at Frau Wolf to sleep for the night. It was impossible to think of falling asleep; they were exhausting hours before the dawn. My suit jacket, ski pants, stockings and red leather slippers, that Wolfhart had given me for Christmas, are stolen. In addition, the photos and film equipment that had been saved up to this point, were dug out from the coal cellar and, of course, taken away. The parents are threatened with being shot.

12th April 1945

Soon after 06.00hrs, I slip quickly back home. Now, I hear everything that has happened, less happily, when you must spend your 20th birthday like this. I can't think of it at all, that today is my birthday! Onkel Josef, Tante Elly, Jochen and Tante Liesel come; on how many years gone by would they come to congratulate me? Instead, everything is so incredibly sad and gloomy in me. Then there's the moving to attend to. Thieving gangs plunder again at Gowin's. We sleep for the first time in the 'new' apartment which resembles a furniture store.

13th April 1945

Relatively quiet. More moving work. Frau Schüster and Fr. Kasper are there to help.

14th April 1945

Moving work. Plundering!! At 13.00hrs, 15.00hrs and around 18.00hrs. Help fetched every time. Adventures with the Russian car! Uschi Pryzemek and Frau Kachel visit us.

15th April 1945

At about 06.00hrs Russian thieving gangs break in again; namely in our cellar and afterwards in Gowin's apartment. Fetched help again. Officers come, driven up by car. No church today on The Lord's Day - there you get snapped up to work. Then the rest of the day quiet.

16th April 1945

Relatively peaceful. Cellar contents moved.

17th April 1945

Nothing shocking happened. We saw remarkably few Russians. Today is your 21st birthday, dear Wolfhart. As a birthday greeting, I adorned a photo of you with colourful spring flowers. Sad that it is already three months that I know nothing more of you. Hopefully, everything will be fine for us.

18th April 1945

Cellar moving again. Onkel Josef helped us with this. At around 22.15hrs, a raid by Russian thieving gangs, always different, new gangs. Until 02.00hrs they romped around. In that way, Mutti's fur coat was also stolen.

19th - 20th April 1945

Relatively quiet.

21st April 1945

Nothing out of the ordinary happened today. Tante Elly and Jochen visit us.

At around 23.00hrs, the windows at Warwas' house are smashed in; Lamla's home is raided.

22nd April 1945

Lord's Day - church at Kreuzkirche. Quiet settles on the day. Mutti and Onkel Josef go to Stroppendorf, on the western outskirts of Gleiwitz. The walk was worth it. Tante Liesel and Uschi Przemeck visit us.

23rd - 25th April 1945

Quiet days. Jochen's birthday 25th April. Went to see him with Mutti. There, I see the Russian quarters - the 'robbers' den.'

26th April 1945

Onkel Joseph, Frau Kachel and Uschi Przemeck are here. Otherwise, all quiet.

27th April 1945

The parents get some garden land near Hallas' apartment, by the old radio transmitter and start digging right away.

28th April 1945

Tante Elly and Jochen come by. In the evening, I go with Vater to Richtersdorf to see Herrn Frank, Tante Elly's brother. Here, we hear the first cuckoo's call.

29th April 1945

Lord's Day - Church at Kreuzkirche. Went to Lamla's. All quiet.

30th April 1945

Got up at 06.00hrs. At 06.30hrs, went with Mutti to the hospital on Preüssen Platz. I am seen and examined by Fräulein Dr. Klüber. Must go back in four weeks. Around 15.30hrs we are back at home.

CHAPTER EIGHT

Unsent diary letters by Christa-Maria

Wahrenbrück, 1ˢᵗ April 1945.

My much-loved Parents and Uschi,

If I'll ever get to read these lines again - I don't know.

I've been thinking of writing to you for a long time, of talking to you; to be able to connect with you, despite the distance and maybe the real upheaval......because I don't know if you are still alive. Because of this, I chain myself to you very tightly, so that the goodness you have given me in your self-sacrificing love does not threaten to perish now that we have been completely separated on the outside.

Somehow, I always shy away from starting these diary letters to you. Today, on Holy Easter Sunday, it is not so hard to write. Despite the severity of sadness that weighs on me, on us, I can say, I was able to capture a piece of Easter joy at Mass and communion today, in my sometimes melancholy and gloomy heart. Easter, and the three holy days before, drew me home to you in a particularly strong way. Your Christele commemorated our annual Good Friday walk and was glad she was able to go to Liebenwerda that day and visit the holy grave there. I can safely say that on Good Friday my soul was saddened to death. I really had to cry again. The thought of what happened on Good Friday, as well as the many memories at home connected with this day, brought this sad mood over me. It was a Good Friday like I've never experienced before, because this time I wasn't just standing in front of the Stations of the Cross contemplating Our Saviour's

suffering; this time I was able to feel Our Lord's anxiety more, because in some ways, we walk our own road of suffering. And today is Easter Day. He is risen! He lives! In previous years, by Easter Sunday, Good Friday is forgotten. One is given joy. One also has no troubles or worries. One could go about one's Easter duties without any difficulties and the best care was always taken to ensure everyone's well-being on such a high holiday.

A little of Good Friday will probably stay with me because it is my wish. Despite our holy faith, which helps me and keeps me from despair, all my sorrows don't want to leave my soul. Even if our Journey to the Cross has not yet ended, even if the last station has not yet been reached, we will have, in Christ, the safety of a bright Easter Day. I hold firmly to that belief. Now, we must learn to pray with sincere hearts, even in tough times: Lord, your Will be done.

This is the will of the God of your sanctification.

Hopefully, you stay steadfast in this hardship.

Oh, that we will be allowed to see each other again!

For today I am, in sincere gratitude, your Christele, for whom you have no need to worry.

19th April 1945, Gamnitz (*Czechoslovakia*)

My dearest Sister,

This second letter is yours - it shall be your birthday letter.

Just a week ago today, a lot happened. But first, I wish you God's protection and blessings in your new year of life. (It is a strange feeling to write to you again when I haven't heard anything from you; perhaps the good Lord has already taken you to himself.) On this, your birthday, I put your picture in my locker and decorated it with a flowering branch. In the evening of your birthday, I wanted to talk more with you, my dear, and then actually write this letter.

But it never came about because, during the night between 12th and 13th April, at 02.30hrs I had to leave Wahrenbrück, that had almost become my second home.

(If only you knew how good I've had it in the camp, since, for the last month, the camp leader has no longer been here.)

Because the 'front' was getting ever closer, our camp had to be broken up. The work maids who arrived last week were sent home. Therese F. went to her parents, who had been bombed out in the Glatz district; two others, Erika Dollinger and I were the homeless ones and didn't know where to go. Our good Frau Mohrmann summoned us and gave us a choice; to go to a camp leader's family in Liebenwerda or go with staff by bicycle to northern Germany, to Hamburg (Frau Mohrmann's hometown) under our own responsibility.

Erika said that she had news from an aunt, who went to the Pilsen district of Czechoslovakia, as a refugee, to live with her family. Erika was about to take me with her, because we two faithful friends didn't want to be separated. As nobody wanted to force me to decide, I found myself in a terrible situation. Never has one faced such a crucial decision alone, without any parental support. If I went east, to try and go home, might I be shot or captured by Russians and sent to Siberia! If I went west...? How could I go west? I knew no-one in the west. The camp group wanted to keep me with them. Herr Hoffman and Frau Brauer wanted to stay there, and they only decide, at the last minute, to go north by bicycle. Lots of options to choose from, just don't stay. I decided to go with Erika to Gamnitz, Tachau district, to her relatives, from Neumarld, near Breslau, Upper Silesia. Of course, I had grave doubts as to whether they would even be able to take me in, since Erika's relatives are refugees themselves. I also thought of the material needs that were waiting for us, destitute work maids, out there in the world. We stood in front of Frau Mohrmann's door for twenty minutes, hesitating, undecided and feeling ashamed to ask for a little money. We felt like beggars.

Frau Schoenemann, whom we first had to get out of bed, gave us 123.60RM[15] in a bashful manner, as pocket money and meal allowance. We were able to take the essentials with us, and some RAD clothing. In any case, everything happened so fast. In a dizziness, I quickly packed my things together, I felt like I wasn't myself at all. We then went in the wagon to Wahrenbrück train station, where we bought four tickets to Dresden.

On the crowded concourse, the ticket suddenly fell out of my hand and, as it was pitch dark, I couldn't find it, so had to buy another one for 3RM. In Rühland, we switched trains. In Pristewitz, we couldn't get on the train because it was over-filled with people. We travelled on an open goods wagon as far as Grossenheim, where we had to wait, almost three hours, for the train to Dresden. It was all so crowded. Soldiers helped us so we were able to get on the platform. The journey from Grossenheim to Dresden was wonderful - mountainous heights, blossoming fruit trees, fairy-tale castles and fields delighted the eye, hungry for colour and beauty, not seen for a long time. The evening spring sunshine covered everything in golden warmth. A quiet joy stirred in my heart to see the magnificent, peaceful Nature of God. That was just another work of our eternal God, in defiance of this horrible war, completely unaffected by the little people, thirsting for death and annihilation.

This small joy made one forget, for a fleeting moment, the dark uncertain days ahead. But all too soon one was thrown back into the grey smoke of reality.

As if one were not spoiled for looking at nature's beauty, because as we got closer to Dresden....... Oh, how terrible to see! One destroyed

---

15 RM stands for Reichsmark which was the currency used in Germany from 1924 - 1945. It was replaced by the Deutschmark in June 1948. Between 1945 - 1948, Allied Military Currency was used as a temporary currency in British, American and French zones.The currency situation during this time was complex and varied depending on specific zones.

house after another, piles of rubble on top of one another, where once stood stately buildings. People clambering, scanning shaky, sunken eyes looking for something, someone - anything that remained of their homes and previous lives. Immediately, I thought of the people, their houses and homes, lost; who saw the fruits of their years of work, suddenly turned into nothing; who mourned their dead, finding their own in graves under the rubble, soot and ashes.

Death, annihilation, destruction, misery and distress - that was the work of man.

Man! what are you doing and what has become of you?

The beautiful Dresden train station! How does it look now? The waiting room in which I sat, together with Kathel, on our journey to Wahrenbrück RAD; the huge room now filled with wide eyed people, kicking through the burnt-out charcoal, hoping to find something.

It was impossible to find one's way through the utter destruction of Dresden's large and beautiful, world-renowned train station.

We had to get our travel certificates in Dresden. Difficulties were still being made for us, since the camp had said the reason for travel was a vacation. As a result, no permit would be issued to us.

Young Camp Leader, Isolde Neumeyer then changed the reason for the trip to 'evacuation of the camp'.

We were then granted our travel permits. We were temporarily given a ticket to Eger, Hungary. It was just about noon when we got to Dresden. Thank God there was only a pre-alarm and not full air-raid.

We left Dresden in SFR to the lovely Bad Schandau, Bodenbach (here we had to separate from Thérèse).

(SFR-*Sonderfahrplan, specially scheduled trains used to evacuate citizens and military personnel from cities during the final days of the war.*)

At Aüssig, an air-raid siren which meant we had to go down to a cellar with all our luggage.

From Aüssig, travelled for 19.5hrs to Karlsbad, where we only arrived at half past midnight. On the train to Karlsbad, we sat together with some shady Italian characters. My head rested on our blankets. Soon, I realised that a tired soldier had laid his tired head close to mine. He was a decent chap with whom I had a very reasonable conversation. In the pitch-dark night, we walked from the main station to the lower station, in unfamiliar Karlsbad, with our heavy luggage. Spent a second night sitting in the waiting room. The next day, in a military car with four officers to Marienbad (Chocolate and filled waffles were given to us in the car.) At 13.00hrs on Saturday we got to Marienbad train station by tram. Air-raid alarm twice in Marienbad. In the afternoon we stood for three hours, on the platform, waiting for the train. Due to overcrowding, we couldn't get on the train, so that meant a third night in a waiting room at Marienbad station. Sunday morning, we finally got away. Got off the train in Plan then finally, at 11.00hrs on Sunday morning, when everything was found to be in order, we hiked from Plan to Gamnitz. On the way, Erika and I sat down to rest and fell asleep in the woods, finally reaching her relatives at 15.15hrs on Sunday afternoon. I was welcomed by her family. We had to sleep at the Innkeeper's house (a rather stubborn woman). Erika's aunt feeds us in exchange for our tokens. We're incredibly grateful for that because we have no pot, no wood (here they only use wood for heating), and we could easily not survive.

Now I have no energy to write further.

For today you have enough news.

On Sunday April 22nd, 1945, I'm thinking of you, my dears.

Christa

Gamnitz, Wednesday 25th April 1945.

My Dears,

This day, Jochen's birthday, was always one where we sat happily together with our relatives from Kreidel Strasse. One felt safe and at ease in this familiar circle. I was happy to be with you, Tante Elly and Onkel Josef. I hope you are lucky enough to have survived these dark days. What extraordinary joy there will be, if it is God's Will that we should see each other again. I have a calm feeling and sure hope that my dearest heart's desire will come true again. I will probably live to see the end of the war here in Gamnitz, judging by what is happening every day and the horrible misery one must see, it cannot be much longer.

Children of indiscriminately wandering people walk wearily from village to village, begging for food. Prisoners and convicts make the area unsafe. Wounded soldiers released from the hospital, struggle to move forward. One wants to help and to give, but one hardly has anything oneself and is dependent on the good favour of other people. Also, you can't trust anyone these days; nobody knows who might be behind a German uniform. Fearful for me, some peasants give these aimless wanderers a humble piece of bread. We only see a small part of the misery that is now raging in our Fatherland, since this small village to which we have fled is a good deal away from the traffic and chaos of the war[16]. At least the widowed farmer and his daughter took us in and gave us a mattress each, in the loft, in exchange for working in his fields.

---

16 This diary entry ended with no sign off or greeting. Gamnitz became home to thousands of German civilian refugees who, like Christa-Maria, were fleeing the ever-advancing Russian Army. Living conditions were dire, with little food, water or medical supplies. In order to survive, Christa- Maria worked on farms digging potatoes and turnips.

CHAPTER NINE

Armistice Day for Ursula

1st May 1945

Morning parade of Russian soldiers with singing and waving of red and white flags.

2nd May 1945

Russian Army holiday, but reasonably quiet. Around 20.30hrs, Herr Hertel is picked up by a Russian officer, guard and interpreter.

3rd May 1945

Polish holiday. Quiet day. Herr Hertel came back around midday. Tante Elly and Jochen come to visit.

4th May 1945

04.30hrs Norbert Schymüra died. Quiet day.

Tante Liesel came, and in the evening, we prayed the rosary for Norbert, with his family at their home.

5th May 1945

Onkel Josef and Jochen here. Alarming Newsflash! Men aged up to 65 years and women up to 55 years must go to Heydebreck[17] for fourteen days to dismantle machines. Rosary said for Norbert at Schymüra's. At night, I watch a gang of robbers break into Frau Strachotta's apartment through the kitchen window at 16, Katzler Strasse.

6th May 1945

The Lord's Day. Church at Kreutzkirche. Quiet day. Rosary at Schymüra's flat.

7th May 1945

Requiem and burial of Norbert Schymüra at the Central Cemetery. In the morning, Polish are there rummaging through things on the streets, in deserted, burnt-out homes, looking for food. Otherwise, quiet.

8th May 1945

Armistice! So, the war should be over?

General Field Marshall Wilhelm Keitel of the Wehrmacht High Command and Chief of Staff General Alfred Jodl offered to surrender.

(First news about the fate of our seducers: Goebbels, his wife and six children, poisoned; Goering caught. And Hitler??? Six corpses from him.)

---

17 Heydebreck was a village close to Gleiwitz where POW and forced labour camps were situated. There was a substantial petrochemical industry here which had been bombed by RAF and USAAF in the 'Oil Campaign" during the night of February 21st- 22nd 1945. The dismantling of machinery was carried out to prevent chemical facilities from getting into Allied hands and/ or destroy evidence of war crimes.

9th May 1945

Tante Liesel and Uschi Przemeck here. In the afternoon, a run in with Dombrowska from the housing commission - an outrageously impudent woman, who speaks German well - a Pharisee type - lying subject, I will not let her in! After that I go with Uschi to see Curate Schenk.

10th May 1945

Ascension Day - Church at Kreutzkirche. A quiet day. I go with Mutti at 19.00hrs to school monastery for May prayers in Latin!! Dombrowska and Stolasski, also one of 'this kind' collect dance records from our flat for their dance evening.

Onkel Josef and Frau Katchel here.

11th May 1945

Quiet day (Americans to occupy Germany????!!)

12th May 1945

Quiet day. Fr. Kasper visits us.

13th May 1945.

Lord's day - church at Kreutzkirche. Glorious, peaceful Sunday. Onkel Josef here.

14th May 1945

Gloomy mood: parents dig in potato field behind Goritzka's house. I wonder if they will reap anything from it. Polish militia at Schymüra's house - big noise.

15th May 1945

Quiet. Parents keep digging. Onkel Josef, Tante Liesel, Tante Anni and Frau Skorrei here.

16th May 1945

Quiet day. Frau Kachel there.

17th May 1945

Quiet day. Uncle Josef and Jochen here. I go with them to see the twins. They then go with me on the way home as far as All Saints' Church where I listen to May devotions in Polish.

18th May 1945

Quiet day, therefore, I go visiting with Mutti - Frau Ziegert, Uschi Przemeck, Tante Liesel and Gottschalk at the Schlesischer-Hof Hotel.

19th May 1945

Quiet. Parents go to Hallas' in the afternoon to dig our patch of garden.

20th May 1945

Whitsunday Church at school monastery. Frauen Kachel, Jendrich and Schüster here.

21st May 1945

Whit Monday - Church at Kreutzkirche. In the morning Frau Ziegert and Frau Juge visit us. Shortly after lunch Vater goes to Stroppendorf with Onkel Josef. Frau Kachel and Uschi Przemeck come by in the afternoon.

22nd - 23rd May 1945

Quiet days. Late afternoon on 23rd May, I go with Mutti to the Central Cemetery, because it is Trautel Lamla's birthday today. Encounter someone from Elsterwerde, and we hear that Russians invaded this area on 22nd - 23rd April. Where might Christel be? Who was still at Bad Liebenwerda? (*Elsterwerde is a town 11km southeast of Wahrenbrück, where Christa-Maria was at RAD camp.*)

Hopefully, we will hear from her again soon.

24th - 26th May 1945

Quiet days. On 25th May we do laundry. Onkel Josef and Frau Kachel visit us.

Vater travels to Ascher on 26th May. Uschi Przemeck comes to me again with all sorts of treasures. (*Ascher, now known as Oświęcim, Poland, is 50km from Gleiwitz.*)

27th May 1945

Lord's Day Church in Kreutzkirche. Onkel Josef, Jochen and Frau Kachel visit us.

I go with Mutti to the school monastery for May devotions.

28th May 1945

In the morning, the Warwas family return from their 'January fleeing' from Rückers in the Glatz district (*Lower Silesia*) and make themselves at home with us.

29th - 30th May 1945

Quiet days. Dombrowska, from Housing Commision, is upstairs because of Polish billeting. Disturbance and agitation. I feel uneasy.

31st May 1945

Corpus Christi - Church at the school monastery. On our house door, there were labels with confirmed Polish residents. Trüdel Hackenberg visited us unexpectedly. She came from

Altewaltersdorf-Habelschwerdt to see her ruined apartment. Onkel Josef and Frau Kachel here. Went with Mutti and Uschi Przemeck to the last May devotions at the school monastery.

Met Fräulein Erdhütter there. (*Fräulein Erdhütter was one of Ursula and Christa-Maria's teachers at the Eichendorff Oberschule, in Gleiwitz.*)

CHAPTER TEN

Christa-Maria's diary letters from Gamnitz

Gamnitz. 20th May 1945.15.00hrs

Pentecost Sunday. Mother's Day.

Written upstairs in the attic, sitting in the poor light that the little window lets in.

My beloved Mother,

The Forget-me-not that I, for your day of honour, have glued in here, lies between the pages of this book, to be pressed. Early this morning on the way to church, I thought of you, my dear Mother, just to put this little flower here because I can't put a fresh May bouquet into your hand myself or give you a heartfelt kiss on your lips.

(I feel the chaos is constricting my throat and my eyes are filled with tears as I write)

If only I could be with you right now! We would both not believe the joy!

I do not give up the hope that our good God will bring us together again.

The sudden end to the war will perhaps allow us just that, to see it come true.

Ah, yes... the end of the war. For two or three days, I walked around as though defeated - the fate that befell our German Fatherland did not escape me. It suddenly woke in me a patriotic feeling I had not actually felt before. It was by no means pity for the sudden end of the National Socialists; rather, I saw the beauty of the German people, as one might experience them in the great spirit of the Fatherland. I am thinking in particular of our most important poets, of linguists and others and it came to my mind that we will try to bury all of this by any means; that there will hardly be a German book; that in schools everything that is genuinely German will be consciously omitted; that one will not be allowed to hear immortal music of great German masters for a long time; and all this because of almost six years of bitter struggle. In every human being, it is like a big mess, everything is agitated and shaken anew. One becomes a big question mark oneself and looks helplessly, with confused eyes, at the turbulent world, also at one's own world, which does not remain unaffected by such gloomy events. You too will surely not have been spared heavy hearts and in the future, you will still wrestle with many more. I know that you certainly don't let anyone know how you feel about it. I believe overall that we often have the same thought and we have shied away from revealing our thoughts to each other. If you can read these lines again, the light will bring tears to your eyes, just like mine.

If only I could call to you: Don't worry about me too much.

Now I can write no further because Fräulein Maritsch came over and is now talking, so I am distracted.

With all sincere gratitude, I think of my beloved Mutti today.

Don't forget me.

Until we see each other again,

Your Christele.

To My Mother.

I would have loved to make a beautiful song,

About your love, your faithful way

The gift that always watches over others,

I would have loved to make it in your honour.

But as I intended to write more,

And as I began to make rhymes,

The floods of the heart surged over it,

Spoiling the delicate waves of the song.

So, accept my simple and plain gift,

Carried by simple and unadorned words,

And take my whole soul within it.

Where one feels most, one doesn't have to say much.

(Inspired by the poem, 'An Meine Mutter' by Annette von Droste-Külshoff 1797 - 1848)

29th May 1945, Gamnitz.

From early morning, same as yesterday, the entire day spreading manure on a huge field of the Meierhof. (*Meierhof refers to a large farm owned by a noble family or wealthy landowner and managed by a steward or overseer.*)

I have two blisters on my left hand. Late in the afternoon, I read something by Schopenhauer, about the value of personality, from an 8th year class book of Fräulein Maritsch.

'It is not crucial what one has, rather who one is.'

31st May 1945. Gamnitz, Feast of Corpus Christi.

My Beloved Parents and Best Sister,

After many years, today is again a real feast day. A rest day in the middle of the week - one is not used to that at all; because the war demanded work, day and night, Sundays and feast days. Perhaps this terrible war must have come so the Holy Church in our German Fatherland can strengthen again. Should we be offering a sacrifice for the victory of our faith? Please don't think I can be easily consoled about what was happening and ignore it. Only today, the first time again at a church service, with plaintive singing and terrible devotions of the villagers who, by their ordinary outward appearance during the Holy Mass, show no inner sympathy at all. I had to think of the prayer unity at our intimate chapel at home and of the tender, melodious, careful and indulgent festive singing from the young faithful throats. I could not find the right devotion in this environment today. From time to time, a few convulsively held back tears, rolled down my face. And I thought of you, my dearests, and of my earlier childhood when Uschele and Christele made their own flower sprays.

If only we could find each other again! I was horrified by the more rural people at the village Corpus Christi Procession.[18] Lord, forgive me if one names the whole thing 'Theatre'. We went home. To me, this procession seemed to be degrading; the surrounding villagers just wanting an excuse to come together. They have their wardrobes out and so much to tell each other. The boys are looking over each other. One hardly wants to know what all the priests in front are full of - one hardly wants to know that! My heart blossoms when I see and live such a Catholic thing as this, and I think of home. For several days I have been plagued by terrible inner doubts. I struggle for the truth within myself. What am I anyway?

---

18 Other opportunities for celebration, partying and dancing were often linked with Church festivals. In late May/June 1945, the Catholic Corpus Christi processions could take place unhindered once again, the route decorated with flower garlands and bouquets. A reason for villagers and towns people to gather and celebrate after the oppression and banning of religious practices during the war years.

Sometimes, it seems to me, my earlier life has disappeared into thin air; as though I had enjoyed a look into a life I was not entitled to.

I often don't even know how I should behave in this environment, to appear genuine to myself. Recognising oneself is the hardest thing. I also have no one here that I can confide in or share my inner doubts with - I am completely by myself and I must deal with that alone. Questions arise in me that I cannot answer by myself. To what extent are perseverance and courtesy, consideration and decency, truthful? It's also in Faust itself: in German, if you're polite, you lie. I also keep asking myself, "Why is one man poor and the other man rich?" One always strives for more, for appearance and prosperity. I also have a very bleak future ahead of me. I know nothing. What shall I do this time, to be what I really am? (If only I knew what I am.) Perhaps you are saved from this internal turmoil. But I certainly don't think it's necessary to go through such conflicts. It's safe to say that nobody talks about it. Between two souls, the same thing often happens; one guards their thoughts from the other to be hidden from them. Hopefully, after this darkness, follows light.

For today I will finish, as it's getting a bit noisy around me.

Today, I am, in love and gratitude,

Your Daughter,
Christa-Maria.

CHAPTER ELEVEN

Polish rule for Ursula in Gleiwitz

1st - 2nd June 1945

Quiet days, nothing happened.

3rd June 1945

Lord's Day - Church at Kreutzkirche. On the way home, I meet Käthie Scholpe and her sister. They have come back from their exile and can't get themselves settled again, especially as Mansfield Strasse, except for a single house, is burnt out. So, it will be for those, who left in January and are now returning, to see our city in ruins.

Herr Birken, who made his way back from the German People's Army to Gleiwitz on an adventurous hike, came to visit us. Early afternoon, Vater visits Onkel Josef. When he returns, Mutti and I go to see Tante Liesel.

4th June 1945

Today the Polish billeting of private persons is supposed to start - thank God it hasn't happened yet. It's downright harassment to billet another of the master race in the already smaller apartment, which, with the furniture of a five roomed apartment in it, looks like a warehouse. Uschi Jendralski visits me today.

5th June 1945

Mutti must go to the Polish district doctor tomorrow because of her work assignment.

I go quickly to Inge Ziegert to get a small bunch of flowers. Onkel Josef visits.

Around 20.00hrs, Polish billeting officers make an appearance.

6th June 1945

In the morning I am alone because Mutti has gone to the German/American Dr. von Botticher (Löseh Strasse, Gleiwitz). Just after noon, Tante Liesel comes - Oma Herbst (Anna) has died at 12.00hrs. "Grant unto her eternal rest....and be a rich reward to her."

Billeting leaves today but wants to come again tomorrow.

7th June 1945

Dombrowska, from the housing committee, sends an older couple from Poland to us for an overnight stay. Onkel Josef here. I visit Inge again.

8th June 1945

Oma Herbst's burial. Afternoon, Mutti goes to Frau Przybilla where she hopes to get some vegetables. My dear friend Uschi Przemeck is leaving me today. She is on the travel document of Trüdel Hackenberg and will travel with her to Patschkaü. She will stay at her grandmother's with her mother and brothers, Eberhard and Klaus. Will we ever see each other again, dear Uschi? I think fondly of the days when we were allowed to sit together in Class 8, right in front of the teacher's desk in the first row of tables. Or should I say, we were told to sit there. Above all, I think of the farewell party and the wonderful summer Sundays on the River Oder in Bischof Forest. Lord God, continue to bless you, who were so courageous and brave, in the grim times now behind us, and had to endure everything alone.

Bye! With a friendly goodbye kiss from your duet partner.

Poland is moving. We are alone.

9ᵗʰ June 1945
Quiet day.

10ᵗʰ June 1945
Lord's Day - church at Kreuzkirche. Jochen came by in the morning. Vater and Onkel Josef in Stroppendorf. I lie down the entire day.

11ᵗʰ June 1945
Quiet day. Frau Kachel here in afternoon.

12ᵗʰ June 1945
Nothing out of ordinary happened. Onkel Josef and Tante Liesel here. Other than that, Herr Heinrich from the District Office here. (German police officers should have been here.)

13th June 1945

Frau Hallas must leave her house today. In the afternoon, I go for a short visit to Ziegert's. In the evening there is frenzied activity clearing our apartment. Sewing backpacks through the night.

14th June 1945

Still restless during the day because of all the clearing. Towards the evening, good news again. (Hair washed.)

15th June 1945

Incident with Frau Wieland - she is taken from her four little children by Polish militia armed with rubber truncheons.

16th June 1945

Quiet. Frau Kachel here in the afternoon.

Around 18.00hrs, Fräulein Erdhütter comes to us to stay overnight and to stay for a day due to an unwelcome incident at the District Office. Then I went to the Wieland children with bread and red fruit jelly. Frau Wieland is safely back again. We are alone until Monday, thank God. (I have a bath today.)

17th June 1945

Lord's Day. Church at the school monastery with Fräulein Erdhütter. There we see Rosemarie Ledwon, a classmate of Christa's who is back from her RAD. In the afternoon, Frau Kachel came with coffee beans; Fräulein Barchfeld asked after Fräulein Erdhütter and according to her, everything is fine on the Leipzig Strasse. Together then we drink the fresh bean coffee. There is even birthday cake! Tante Liesel visits and I go to see Inge.

18th June 1945

Today we're celebrating Mutti's birthday; you could say, like never before. Dear Mutti, let me wish you God's blessings sincerely, His constant support this year too, health and very soon, news of Christel. Everything will be fine again soon. Tante Anni, Frau Hutter, Tante Liesel and Onkel Josef here. We hear all sorts of new things. (Vater goes with Fräulein Erdhütter to a Polish Course.)

19th June 1945

Fräulein Erdhütter went home this morning. Big disturbance with clearing in Katzer apartment at 10.00hrs, 12.00hrs and 14.00hrs. Frau Hüttner is thrown out of her apartment, she comes to us to sleep. In the evening Mutti goes to Frau Kachel, who has had news of Ruth from Habelschwerdt.

20th June 1945

Relatively quiet. Frau Kachel came by. Frau Hüttner sleeps another night with us.

Late afternoon I visit Inge Ziegert.

21st June 1945

Passed peacefully.

22nd June 1945

Towards evening I visit Inge again. Herr and Frau Schüster visit us.

Her fate is also a sad one.

23rd June 1945

Passed quietly.

24th June 1945

Lord's Day. Church at the school monastery. Learn from Curate Schenk that Alice Pifko, History Teacher from Eichendorff Oberschule, should be there. (In the morning there are Polish propaganda processions and occupation of barracks by Polish military.)

Frau Hüttner comes to sleep at our apartment. But she still goes with Vater to the Russians she knows about our trip to the German side, since it is impossible for us to survive under the harshness of Polish rule.

25th June 1945

Peaceful! Mutti did laundry. I went to Inge Ziegert, then we went together to Frau Przybilla to fetch vegetables and berries for Vater.

We have an encounter with German Soldiers!!!

26th June 1945

Lamla's were turfed out of their home today. I went with Mutti to Tante Liesel, Onkel Josef, Fraulein Erdhütter and Liane, who is back from her RAD and from whom we hope to learn something about Christa. In our absence Inge Ziegert comes; we want to leave together so we're packing.

27th June 1945

In the afternoon, German soldiers come from work, passing by us, singing 'The Blue Dragons - Heidemarie'. Onkel Josef and Inge Ziegert visit us.

28th June 1945

Quiet. In the afternoon, furtively passed blancmange pudding to passing German soldiers with a little verse.

'Every day I see you pass by,

probably thirty men in rows of three.

For your German song, heard yesterday,

for the first time in six months,

This gift is a small thank you.

Enjoy the 'water pudding' [19]and

always have cheerful courage.

Better times will come again,

When all misery will finally be taken from us,

Next time, if it's possible, sing:

'There is a mill in the Schwarzwald valley.'

Your

U.C

---

19 The blancmange pudding powder would have been mixed with water instead of milk or cream, which were rarely available. The song, 'There is a mill in the Schwartzwald valley' is a traditional German folk song.

Went to school monastery; met Susi Sommer there. Go with Mutti to Fräulein Broll, who had a car to go across to the German side, an opportunity, but in vain.

29th June 1945

Saint Peter and Saint Paul's feast day. Church at 08.30 hrs. Liane came this morning. Parents are on a car finding mission. Tante Liesel is again upstairs. In the evening I went to see Inge Ziegert.

30th June 1945

Nothing happened in the morning. Frau Korra was thrown out of her apartment in the afternoon. Susi Sommer gets potatoes and sauerkraut - they have nothing left to eat. (Vater, by way of example, buys sausage with Polish money. I eat two frankfurters for 44Pf. - German money.) Frau Hüttner sleeps at ours again.

CHAPTER TWELVE

Christa-Maria's Trek begins

The village of Gamnitz in Czechoslovakia, where Christa-Maria fled with her school friend Erika, was in rural isolation at the end of WW2 in May 1945. The American Army arrived from the west to liberate the Czech people from Nazi occupation. There is no diary entry for this, but from conversations with my mother, I know Gamnitz was a small farming village situated on the banks of a lake. A village so small, it had no shop, no church and no military barracks. Christa-Maria went to a neighbouring village to attend Mass on Sundays when she could. She remembers hearing the approaching soldiers, firing their rifles, not knowing if they were Russian or American. Christa-Maria hid in the farmer's cellar with Erika, her family and other refugees waiting anxiously in the cramped, dark space while the community leader was walking towards the soldiers, waving a white handkerchief tied, in two places, to a slender branch. In English, Christa-Maria explained to the soldiers peering down the trap door, they were just farmers and refugees, not a weapon between them. Some had fled Upper Silesia, in the bitter January cold, their possessions piled high on wooden horse drawn carts, over the Sudetenland Mountains. The Americans were kind, distributing tinned food, water and medical supplies to the refugees. They moved on after a few *days, returning some weeks later offering protection from potential Russian attacks, as they were told to make their way home. Known as The Trek, Christa-Maria and Erika began their hike back to Germany, with hundreds of other refugees in the week 11 - 18th June 1945. With American soldiers to guide and protect them, they began walking, alongside open hand carts and pack horses, through forests, open countryside and over the Eastern Ore mountains setting up camp where they could, in the hope of reaching the German border. On occasion, an army jeep had to haul a cart full of possessions up the difficult, steep terrain.*

This group of refugees was just a small fraction of the millions of Germans who were displaced, being neither where they belonged nor wanted to be - 9 million bombed-out, 14 million refugees and exiles, 10 million released forced labourers and countless millions of slowly returning prisoners of war. Infrastructure was destroyed and there was no postal service, causing chaos for starving, homeless people desperate to re-connect with relatives and find a place to settle in safety. When refugees moved from place to place, they left notes on walls and doorways detailing who they were and where they were trying to get to. Urgent messages were left with the people staying behind in the hope of information being passed on to the next influx of refugees. Somebody, somewhere must know the person being searched for in all the chaos! This was their only way to network and connect with people from their hometowns, who might know the whereabouts of a missing relative. During long, fractured journeys, Christa-Maria criss-crossed the broken country on foot, weighed down with the few belongings she could carry, in columns of people with hand carts or on cramped freight trains, sleeping in waiting rooms, tunnels and ditches surrounded by the detritus and ruins of war. Anything in which to carry belongings became a most desirable item; suitcases were often stolen from beside their exhausted, sleeping owners. When they arrived at the German border, the American convoy dispersed, and Christa-Maria was bundled on to an open freight train going where? She did not know.

Sunday 10th June 1945, Gamnitz.

Church Fair in Gamnitz. The Pastor was two hours late, so there were few people in the chapel because most were having lunch. People are very naughty to put eating before praying! In the afternoon, with three elderly ladies, I went singing in a Czech's back garden. Songs from the Spielmann with loud accompaniment. Now, I am lying outside on a green field. I didn't eat the last two days because I sprained my right foot and couldn't work. No work, no food! It is now very bruised, and the doctor ordered a few days bed rest, but - well with the farm, there's just too much work and I didn't want to be a burden to the people. I didn't want to be any trouble. Miss Maritsch was friendly, and although I didn't work, she got something for me to eat, and that was a fine feeling.

18th June 1945, Mutti's birthday.

Outside and on the Trek.

My beloved Mutti,

What can I say to you, my dearest Mutti?

If you could see me here...... but today I will not talk about me so much, even if it be of great interest to you.

Today is your day of honour - your birthday, a wonderful summer's day, a day filled with God's beautiful nature; rich light, swaying back and forth through cornfields decorated with red poppies; the lush, tall meadow grass fallen under the swing of the peasant woman's scythe. A day made in your honour.

It would seem a little shallow, if I were just to write, 'I wish you a warm Happy Birthday.'

So today rather, I think the entire day of our Lord God and thank him, sincerely from my heart, for giving me such a Mutti as you. Only now, that I experience so many people and families (especially on the trek, you do get to know people well) do I truly realise what you, my parents, have given me. Even when I hear many a bad word or expression about the Truth, I can proudly say: 'I never heard such a thing from my Mutti!' I also pray today for all my loved ones. I think back to your 50th birthday and the Holy Mass in the chapel at home. You will certainly understand that tears well up in my eyes with these happy memories, my dear Mutti, since you are the one who understands me best and most warmly in all things. I ask the dear Lord God, if it is his holy Will, that he may bring us together again. I know you feel as I do, when I say this prayer, and you can sympathise with me. I can't say these words without a tremble of my lips, my eyelashes and cheeks wet with tears. Oh, my dearest Mutti! Would that I could be with you and pour my heavy heart out to you! A thousand heartfelt thanks for your love and goodness. Oh, can I repay you a little for the love you have shown and that you didn't show anger to me when I have saddened you sometimes. If I had been able to guess how many a harsh word might have offended your kind heart, I would not have done it.

Why do people finally see and understand things properly when it is too late?

My dearest Mutti, on the Trek, I pinned a violet, wildflower to my RAD wind jacket (violet - your favourite colour) and a pale blue forget-me-not. Today, I will place a loving, tearful kiss on your picture. Something beautiful from my treasure chest, which I was able to enrich quite a bit in Gamnitz, will I write for you at the end of this birthday letter. I have never had to send you private birthday greetings before because I have always been with you, my dearest Mutti. And today? Today these lines can't even reach you. Oh, poor heart! Don't be afraid - everything, everything will turn around.

On your 51ˢᵗ birthday, your dear child thinks of her good and loving Mutti.

Christa.

'Shatten sind des Lebens güter,

Schatten seiner Freuden Schar

Schatten Worte, Wünche, Talen.

Die gedanken nür sind Wahr.'

Translation:

'Shadows are the goods of life,

Shadows of its joys abound,

Shadows of words, wishes, tales,

Only thoughts are truly sound.'

Franz Grillparzer (1791 - 1872)

22ⁿᵈ June 1945

Pichl auf der Wiese.

I struggled to find where/what Pichl auf der Wiese meant in the context of this diary. It is place in the Styrian region of Austria. However, based on the movement of The Trek and the places mentioned in this section of Christa-Maria's diary, my interpretation of Pichl auf der Wiese is the literal translation, 'a clearing in the meadow.' She describes sleeping on open carts in the forest as the Trek moved on from Gamnitz. I don't think she knew exactly where she was as they made camp where they could, moving under cover of the forest, through a mountainous area that is now known as the Karlovy Vary region of the Czech Republic.

Yesterday, I walked for an hour and, from 08.30hrs till after midday, I queued for bread.

I have a slice with me. A dry crust from the bread that was shared out along with peas, mashed potato, salt, sugar, coffee, canned meat and dried onions from the Americans.

I have never waited so long for bread in my whole life!

I played interpreter - an American came with the trek leader and wanted bread.

If I hadn't translated, the whole bread would have been confiscated and we would have had to wait another 5 hrs to get more, if at all. On the way home, I got thoroughly soaked and, because of the severe weather, we all had to huddle together in the small, full wagon, adopting any possible or impossible position of steadiness to eat our soup and first fresh lettuce! Mutti! Mutti! If you could see me like this!

Sunday 24ᵗʰ June 1945 (Feast of John the Baptist) Pichl

I lie in the summer forest. The little birds chirp to one another from the swaying treetops. Had a wonderful time sleeping in the good forest air. Earlier at 08.30 am, went to Mass in Lichtenstein, wearing the blue dress that I wore to the Czech First Communion celebrations. I remembered my own First Communion with a strong memory. I had to shed some tears.

(Lichtenstein, not to be confused with the small landlocked country in Central Europe, Liechtenstein, is known today as Líštany in the Plzeň region of the Czech Republic.)

25ᵗʰ June 1945

Hair and combs washed in forest. Collected wood (kindling).

Rained in the morning.

Tuesday 26ᵗʰ June 1945

Today, one week in Pichl.

Americans came with copious amounts of insecticide for body crawling insects. They spray everyone with this large spray thing - on the head and back, on clothes, under clothes and armpits. The soldiers noticed that I could speak English and kept me there as a helper. One talked little as soldiers are not very clever. I was given a box of the powder for helping. Saw some very 'lousy' heads!

In the evening I had blueberries for the first time this year - with sugar and two dry slices of bread.

After supper, I gathered wood in the forest.

Wednesday, 27th of June 1945, 21.oohrs. Pichl

In Lichtenstein to get vinegar and salt. Came home with enormous hunger.

Found a few cherries on the way and shook some down from a tree. The temptation was too great!

Erika went to a house to ask for a little piece of bread - we were rejected rather abruptly!

For lunch, we had flour dumplings and blueberry dip.

It rained in the afternoon. Six of us sat crooked and crumpled in the little wagon. Cold. Had to put on some knitwear. New Americans came today; the old ones went away.

Goodnight, my dearest parents and Uschi.

Thursday 28th June 1945. Pichl

Oh, my dearests! I so much want to be with you! I could howl.

Today, it is so cold that I had to wear track pants, jacket and winter coat in Lichtenstein. Got 50 grams of margarine. Got back at 15.3ohrs. Erika and I no longer feel comfortable in these surroundings. Too much conflict and constant bickering around us. Our refuge is then usually the quiet deep forest where only the gentle chirping of birds can be heard.

I am so sad; no roof over my head, no bed to sleep on, little bread, no Mutti, no Papa, no sister; no-one that I can pour my heart out to. I just feel so isolated.

Oh, dear God! Help me!

29th June 1945. St Peter & St Paul Feast Day

Went to church at 08.00hrs

On the way back, found many cherries under the tree. Freezing cold. Had to wear winter clothes, I was so cold. There is no way to get warm! Ach! Can't I come home to you?

Saturday 30th of June 1945, Pichl

Dug potatoes from a stack - 70kg.

Blessed bread.

Ate cherries.

Chapter Thirteen

Ursula leaves her home

1st July 1945, Lord's Day

Church at school monastery, Frau Kachel there. Herr Heinrich came; he wants to turn up again in the afternoon. We finish our preparations for our journey to the German side. I go with Mutti to Curate Schenk. We bring him some useful things for the monastery's business from our household.

2nd July 1945

Curate Schenk wanted to come to us at 11.00hrs but we weren't there. Herr Heinrich is upstairs. A black day, we should have left today but it has been delayed. Inge Ziegert here. Frau Hüttner came to sleep. A Polish man came with his wife to stay the night.

3rd July 1945

We should receive notice from Herr Heinrich today. Vater went to Curate Schenk today. He will come this afternoon and is with us by 13.00 hrs. He takes the cine camera, some books and photo albums, along with some other things that he will keep for us, for as long as we need him to. Tante Liesel and Jochen came to pick up some things.

4ᵗʰ July 1945

By midday, still no notice from Herr Heinrich. Frau Ziegert here. Frau Hüttner comes again to sleep. Around 21.00hrs we hear final rejection from Herr Heinrich.

Vater sold the vacuum cleaner in the Polish quarter.

5ᵗʰ July 1945

Vater was not at home early this morning. Polish (Lieutenant Borowski and two women) drive up and want to go straight to our apartment. They only speak Polish, and we can't understand a word - they take a close look around our apartment. Will one of the women become the owner of our furniture??? By the time Vater gets back, it's all over. He had negotiated a price for the sunlamp with an American doctor, then he went over to Onkel Josef's house where he met a friend with whom he spoke about the car journey to the German side. Mutti goes to Curate Schenk with the rolled-up oil painting and some other things.

6ᵗʰ July 1945

We're busy packing the necessary things - it will be a long time before we have the joy of being in our own apartment again. Stolarski took our record cabinet with all the records from here. No point being sad when something like this happens. We're allowed to own nothing. Frau Hüttner here to sleep.

7th July 1945

Relatively quiet. In the evening, we manage, with Mutti, to take some crystal ware to Curate Schenk, while the house is unguarded. Frau Hüttner here to sleep. Today the fridge is taken from us by another Pole. Mean dog!

8th July 1945

Lord's day. Church at school monastery. Mutti and I take some more crystal to Curate Schenk. And my briefcase. Around midday, I go once more to Curate Schenk with things. In the afternoon Gisela Jendralski and Külli came by. Gisela and I carry a featherbed to her place for 'safekeeping'. Incident with Hampe and Polish militia while I was away. One more visit to Curate Schenk, who wants me to stay with him at the monastery overnight, to sleep. Since the parents didn't have any knowledge of this plan, I rushed home because there is still so much to do. Frau Hüttner with us to sleep.

9th July 1945

I got up early. At 11.30hrs the Polish housing people appeared - we must leave the apartment in ten minutes - given a room in the German Ghetto. Frau Ziegert happened to be upstairs with Inge - they help us. Mutti and I fetch a cart to load our luggage, while Vater must protect the last of our belongings from Russians, who pounce on them like vultures. With our belongings, we walk through the streets, towards the monastery. On the way, we go through Polish Control to be accounted for, but that goes well. "Operation survived, patient alive," is how Curate Schenk greets me. For the time being, Mutti and I will be accommodated in the kindergarten.

Vater stays with Oncle Josef - they go to fetch Christel's case from the Goritzka-Strohschober apartment building in the evening.

10th July 1945

Sister Imelda comforts us in the morning, then Curate Schenk takes pity on us and offers Mutti and me his living room.

I must lie down on his couch; I am not up to it. Until Curate Schenk comes back to his apartment, (he's on his way) I can lie down. Inge Ziegert was thrown out by Russians today. While I help her carry a few things, Poles rob us on the street.

We sleep together in the kindergarten.

11th July 1945

I helped in the monastery kitchen, otherwise nothing special.

We're supposed to move on in the evening but sleep another night in the kindergarten.

Kreuzkirche is desecrated, thereby we lose our stamp album - a valuable item, that could have helped us out over many things.

12th July 1945

We're moving to the Gartenhaus today - Room 8.

The parents are not allowed in our old apartment.

13th July 1945

Nothing special happened. Parents still can't go back to the apartment. In the evening, Vater tried again one more time; he met Udritzki, who gave him meat and bread.

14th July 1945

Saturday work in the monastery kitchen, washing salad and turnips. In the afternoon I go with Mutti to Frau Ziegert's where we drink coffee - there is Streuselkuchen!!!!

15th July 1945

Lord's Day. Church at the school monastery at 08.00hrs. Mass offered for Archbishop Cardinal Adolf Bertram, from Breslau, who died 8th July 1945. Dear God, let him rest in peace. Amen.

At 12.00hrs we go to Onkel Josef for dinner. Vater brings the meat from Udritzki and Tante Elly prepares it. Drank coffee with Ziegert family in the courtyard at the monastery. I get things out of the suitcase to sell on the black market.

16th July 1945

Fr. Maniera from Berlin is here. He says mass in school monastery. In the cloister, intruding militia snatch Mutti and Frau Ziegert to work in the yard. I ran away quickly. I washed some clothes, baked some bread. Around midday Mutti and Frau Ziegert are back. I get a message from Uschi Przemeck in Patschkaü through Sister Annetta.

17th July 1945

I help in the monastery kitchen, otherwise nothing special.

18th - 19th July 1945. Quiet days. Fräulein Erdhütter came to visit us in the monastery.

We discuss about the joint departure.

20th - 21st July 1945

Quiet days. I just have terrible toothache and must go to the dentist on both days. It's not too bad - my wisdom tooth is hurting. Also go to Dr. von Bötticher to get my medical certificate.[20]

22nd July 1945

Lord's Day. Church at school monastery. Afterwards, I go with Vater to the Kreutzkirche, that is open again, to ask about the stamp album.

The effort was in vain.

23rd July 1945

About midday, Polish come to monastery looking for SS and Germans. Great agitation and unrest. I go to help with shovelling coal. Meeting of monastery residents with Curate Schenk after our 'examination' by Poles.

24th - 25th July 1945

Quiet days. Sweep the yard with roommates in the evening.

---

20 Ursula's medical certificate is written in Polish, stating thyrotoxicosis as the medical condition exempting her from rubble clearing and other hard, physical tasks. Russians/Polish militia would round up German civilians and force them to do manual labour tasks.

26th July 1945

Tidy the study with roommates. In the evening I go with Vater to 7, Ludendorff Strasse, where I am generously allowed to fetch my essays from the attic.

27th July 1945

Today, I go with Vater to the Schacher[21] market. A terrible picture in front of me.

After midday, Polish came to the flat. Ziegert Family suddenly able to go to Glatz in Russian car. They allegedly had a driver. Hopefully, they got through it all without incident.

28th July 1945

Saturday evening work. Quiet day.

29th July 1945

Lord's Day. Church at school monastery at 08.00hrs. Nothing special happened. In the evening we go to pray for blessings and then we pray with Curate Schenk.

---

21 Jewish survivors of liberated concentration camps, housed in ghettos, ventured into towns where 'Schacher' markets were held. Stolen or looted black market goods and services were traded between Jewish survivors and displaced German refugees, illegally, without money, using bartering as a form of exchange. 'Schacher' is a pejorative term that describes bargaining, haggling, profiteering and extortion.

30th July 1945

Father went to Schacher market again. In the evening we have our last gathering with Curate Schenk.

31st July 1945

Nothing special.

CHAPTER FOURTEEN

Christa-Maria's new job on the Trek

Sunday 1st July 1945, Pichl

Went to Lichtenstein church at 08.30hrs. Very satisfied with the service and participation of the congregation, but still a long way from surpassing our services at the convent chapel at home.

After the meal, unfortunately, wood had to be chopped, because there was only kindling there, and the pancakes need a lot of fire.

Monday 2nd July 1945, written on 3rd July 1945

Terrible weather - spent entire day lying on the wagon. Didn't feel well at all. Was more mentally than physically ill. Onkel Doctor gave me two tablets for a cold. Received food. Never any meat. Only fat scraps.

Tuesday 3rd July 1945

Again, lay in wagon. Feeling awful with headache and terrible longing for home.

Cold rainy weather again - slept nearly all day.

Dear God, put an end to this need! When the weather is so bad, everything comes to my consciousness - no roof over my head, just a leaking carpet.

Keeping the fire going in the open, depends entirely on the weather.

Oh Mutti! Ach! Can I come to you soon?

Wednesday 4th July 1945

Much quarrelling between the two brothers. Torn from the forest. Shed some tears

Great longing for home.

Thursday 5th July 1945. Pichl

Packed and stacked carrots in the barn.

Dr. May has brought us unfortunate news about our prospects of coming home. A few tears have flowed in the solitude of the forest whilst gathering kindling twigs. Went to Poplowitz to beg for a pot this morning. Forgive me. I had to swallow my pride. I was so looking forward to dumplings for lunch. Unfortunately, dumplings were only made for Herr Hentschel. Very cold today. I must wear woollen pants and long tights to keep warm. Dear Mutti, when will I be with you again?

Friday 6th of July 1945. Pichl

Dr. May got me out of bed early this morning to interpret. Two Americans were waiting for me in Dr May's room. Waiting for me! The only one who could enable communication between them. This was my first interpretation for Dr. May. Then I talked a little bit to him and his wife. These are just the people I long for. I mean, the milieu is so different, even if Dr. May is living in a very primitive farmhouse. At lunch time the nurse called me, on behalf of Dr. May, to the Americans. A girl had broken her arm and had to be sent from the Americans to hospital for X-rays. With Erika, wrote out the most necessary vocabulary from the medical dictionaries, to learn it properly. Fresher weather again today.

Saturday 7th July 1945, Pichl

In the late afternoon, as I was stirring the potato soup, Frau Dr. May came and told me to come over to do some interpreting. The American was genuinely nice. He told me a lot about the conditions in Germany. It was remarkably interesting. On behalf of Frau May, I then asked if it would be possible to send mail to her brother, a veterinary professor at a University for Prisoners of War in USA.

When the American had said goodbye to Frau May, I spoke with him alone and asked if he could send a letter to Tante Dorchen in Bielefeld for me. He promised me he would, but I shouldn't tell anyone. I showed him where our wagon was. He said he would come tomorrow, Sunday, or in next few days, to pick up my letters.

Sunday 8th July 1945

Didn't go to church today. Aunt Mia and Mia went to the service. Erika had stomach-ache. I just saw to the kitchen. In the afternoon, invited to the doctors for coffee. The vastly different milieu suited Erika and me very well. They were extraordinarily nice to us. We behaved like young ladies! Instead of a lady's cigarette, Dr. May offered to light us a lady's cigar! He was almost angry when we thanked him and said no. But we didn't refuse the schnapps that was offered afterwards.

Dr. and Frau May drank from a goblet; Erika and I, from a second glass.

Monday 9th July 1945

Translating again. Went to see Onkel Dr. because of my rash. He gave me some salicylic ointment.

In the afternoon, went with Erika to Krutschowitz to get some turnips and horse feed.

Tuesday 10th July 1945

Did laundry. Translating again in the afternoon. An American doctor and chemist were there with a catalogue of medical instruments and medicines. Dr. May marked what he needed. The Americans had little finesse - feet on the chairs, slouched over the tables and left without a word of goodbye. Got a coffee and piece of cake from Frau May. Then went to the forest to pick strawberries with her. We had a nice chat. It suits me very well, when I can be with nice people again. The wild strawberries we collected were given to Lothar.

Wednesday 11th July 1945

Went to see Onkel Dr. about the ointment. The sister bandaged my arm and Dr. May sprayed my leg with something from the Americans. Carrots and pea pods for lunch. Terrible and persistent harsh, wet, weather in the afternoon. Almost the whole meadow under water! Ponds have overflowed.

Thursday 12th July 1945

A catering issue in the morning due to the heavy rain from yesterday afternoon.

Did mending in the afternoon.

Friday 13th July 1945

One year anniversary since my last school day.

I wandered back a year in thought. You, my beloved parents went to Bad Kissingen that day.

Anxious feelings moved us when we said goodbye at the station at noon, in this already critical time. And yet, one could be happy at this time. Another successfully completed school year behind me. You can call yourself a high school graduate. Three beautiful weeks of holiday, the last big holiday, lay ahead of me. I still had a home, which I, unfortunately, only appreciate now that I see how things are in so many other families. Oh, my dearly beloved parents! I could let you feel how much value your upbringing has had, and will have, I could thank you most heartily with fine humble words. It will never be in vain. On that day, 13th July 1944, I had a night watch. I was late because I had chatted too long with Friedbert, who came with me to the school. Our topic of conversation was how Curate Schenk and Frau Walter would be annoyed and upset about me being late. I remember that.

Who would have guessed, back then, what awaited us in the following year? What will happen between now and 13th July 1946? Oh, beautiful past! Could you return once more?

Here, in Pichl, on 13th July 1945, I went to pull turnips. I have no energy for this. I was in a rather gloomy mood because of thinking back a year.

Saturday 14th July 1945, Pichl

Made substantial progress with making my brown skirt, so think will wear it with my blue RAD blouse on Sunday. In the afternoon, repetition of delousing by the Americans. From Frau Dr. May, a little piece of torte to try. My things pressed with an 'economy iron'. Food distributed. Washed and poured a bucket of water over myself in the moonlight on the meadow. It must've been at least 23.00hrs.

Sunday 15th July 1945 Pichl

In Anischau *(Czech Republic - Úněšov)* for Mass. Lovely weather. We went through mature, golden yellow cornfields on our way to church. Sermon, preached well and in a relevant way, about trusting in God. The whole service is satisfactory for village standards. After lunch, looked for raspberries to have with this evening's semolina pudding. Then went into the forest with Erika. Slept for a while first. Then began the book, 'Ja, Vater', by Gräf[22]. It is certainly not by accident that the book is now in my hands. Lord, thank you for that. Went to Frau Dr. May for a short chat in the evening.

Monday 16th July 1945

Called to Dr. May for interpreting in the morning. Two senior officers were there, waiting.

Read 'Ja, Vater'. A hot summer's day.

Thursday 19th July 1945

Left for Tepl. Very troublesome journey and so hot. At dusk we arrived at a meadow.

Adventures with the two Americans on horseback but we renounce their many promises and stick to ourselves. Spoke with four nice Americans in

---

22 'Ja Vater, Alltag in Gott' - a book of daily spiritual reflections by P. Richard Gräf published in 1940.

the meadow under the moonlight. Slept under the stars without anything warm to eat all day, apart from the flour soup we ate this morning.

Friday 20th July 1945

Was raining early this morning so moved into the camp. Two former RAD camps. New barracks are made by German prisoners of war. Lots of Americans in the camp. Washrooms in this RAD camp are the same as in Wahrenbrück. Almost made me feel at home! In the afternoon, at 17.00hrs, received a thin bread soup. Spoke with two Americans in the evening - about Germany, Hitler and so on. One of the Americans had been together with the Russians and refuted our propaganda.

Saturday 21st July 1945. Tepl

(Written on Sunday morning.)

In a tent built out of a carpet, the night was very cold. Washed in the washroom and brought water. Became dull and quiet. Also, something going on with Erika. In the afternoon, camp roll call, where they announced the opportunity to go to confession. In the evening, there was singing practice scheduled, ready for the morning service, if it can take place.

In the afternoon, there were five church ministers. They sat in the forest on chairs, in the middle of the horses, amongst the destroyed barracks that had been built by German soldiers.

The repentant people then knelt on the forest floor, next to the chairs, to make their confession.

I couldn't go. I want a longer chat with a priest and therefore did not want to pour my heart out in the open to a priest I don't know and who doesn't know me. It's quite impressive how religious freedom is suddenly back; how our victors take care of the spiritual, soulful being of the defeated.

One can now realise quite how restricted we were in our religious freedom. I think of the RAD camp at Wahrenbrück. There was a risk, to ask for permission to go to church, and then the 6km walk to Liebenwerda, the early getting up, the complaints of some comrades, who wanted to make snide remarks at us.

And now, now I find myself again in such 'dead' RAD camps and we are appointed five ministers for Saturday confession. On Sunday morning they're already there, 1.5 hours before the divine service. Perhaps we have had to endure all this suffering to regain our religious freedom and bring victory for the Church of God, in Germany.

Went to the forest to collect firewood in the afternoon. At 16.30hrs, we are given food for the first time today. Pea soup - a bowl full for each person, bread shared between two and some meat. Was given half a slice of ham by Frau Hesse. We couldn't go to the shower anymore because it was too late. Before going to bed, still a little unsettled in my thoughts. To bed on the feed wagon, slept on oat bags.

Sunday 22nd July 1945. Lord's Day

Up at 06.45hrs. Peeled potatoes, fetched water, ate semolina, got washed and dressed.

At 09.00hrs went to service in the barracks.

It has pierced me again. Insistently, the refugee people pleading to their God. There was an atmosphere within these wooden walls that made me feel a bit gloomy again. The Holy Mass was held for all the refugees - those living and those now dead, who had belonged to them.

It is understandable that one was there with one's loved ones during the whole Holy Mass, that one was also reminded of the services of worship in the chapel at home. And I think of the last mass with Curate Schenk. We were banished then and have not been able to return since.

In any case, I was so far into my sorrow that I just couldn't hold myself any longer and had to have a good cry. Frau Hesse took me, in a motherly way, under my arm, and quietly told me to go with her to the barracks, where she sat me on the edge of the bed and tried to comfort me.

Slept with Frau Hesse in her bed that night.

Monday 23rd July 1945
Cold. Afternoon roll call. Had potato soup with lots of potato peel in it. Could not eat much.

Fetched firewood. Herr Hesse got me a bed in the barracks - top bunk.

Tuesday 24th July 1945
Cold. Nothing to eat today. Hungry, hungry, hungry! Sat on the bed in the afternoon. Did some darning and writing.

Wednesday 25th July 1945
Used the last of the potatoes for lunch today. Tomato sauce and potatoes. The kitchen only has the same. Four potatoes per person, no bread.

Dr. May came late afternoon with a family and their belongings from Pichl where the camp had been disbanded so Dr. May brought some of the families here. A glimpse of light?

People one had come to love, and we were only separated for a week.

Thursday 26th July 1945

A warm July day. Went to get wood in the forest. Had a whole-body wash in a hidden pond.

Peas and potato cakes for lunch. Camp meal: Unsalted peas.

In the afternoon I read from 'Ja, Vater': Lord, teach us how to pray.

Have again pondered a lot over poor and rich, high and lowly. How come one man is rich, the other poor? What am I? I only want to be what I truly am. But what am I anyway?

Had hiccups today Mutti - were you thinking of me?

Friday 27th July 1945

Did laundry in the afternoon. Rinsed off in the pond. Was very annoyed because Tante Mia had all her family's washing there too. She has a sore thumb, so I have to do all the washing, in the pond, by myself. But the reward of this day was nice; Dr. May had us round to his at 20.00hrs. The two girls, who had been Czech maids, would be hired to help in reception. Dr. Vogel, a young German officer, left for the military hospital in Tepl. Dr. May is the only doctor here at this camp. Both Red Cross nurses went with Dr. Vogel too. Frau Kindell found us some white aprons and caps. Did not sleep very well as had to be up at six to get to Dr. May by 07.30hrs.

Saturday 28th July 1945

Got up at 06.00hrs. Went to the bathing pond to wash. Then our work started.

Sick Americans go in and out of the consulting room. It went very well. Nurse Erika and Nurse Christa did their job very well! The American Major and the Lieutenant were presented with the new nurses. The

Americans go, off and on, into the consulting room. I must thank God that, so far, I have remained healthy, when I have seen so much illness. In the afternoon, I made everything tidy again in the consulting room with Frau Dr. May. It was necessary for someone to be there until after 19.00hrs.

For 3 - 5 hrs in the afternoon the sick came to be bandaged. Practiced bandaging with Frau Dr. May and made muslin swabs.

A lot happened in this day. I am genuinely happy and thankful to have this new sphere of work.

Sunday 29th July 1945, Tepl Camp. Lord's Day

Icy, chilly day. Sunday work so didn't go to church. But I believe in cases like this where, of your own free will, you do something for others, it is acceptable.

Had lunch at Tante Mia's, by her cart - mutton with dumplings - great. Received coffee pudding from Frau Dr. May. God is looking after me.

In today's lesson it also says: 'Cast your cares to the Lord and he will nourish you'.

I sit all by myself in the consulting room and pray from the 10th Sunday after Pentecost text.

Nearby, I can hear a radio that seems to have been on all day where the Americans slouch around.

Monday 30th July 1945

Got up at 06.00hrs. Slept in the consulting room. A great operation in consulting room this morning.

Called to see a girl who had fainted and one who had fallen from the top bunk and split open her bottom lip. Then, I went with Dr. May to the sick in the camp and made gauze swabs. Received some instruction from Dr. May. Visited the future hospital barracks with Dr. May and the American Lieutenant, interpreted for them. Went back to the consulting room for some peace and quiet.

Tuesday 31st July 1945

Very cold! Fewer operations during consultation today. I have such a strange feeling that I can't put it into words.

I need a lot of work clothes for this new sphere of activity. The one blue dress is not enough. I want to be clean and neat, but there are simply not enough resources. I want to wash my hair, no time, no hot water. We have absolutely no time to collect any firewood to wash the white aprons, since, after three days, they are no longer thoroughly clean. Mutti, you would soon wash and iron the aprons for me.

Oh! my dearest Mutti, when will we see each other again?

CHAPTER FIFTEEN

Ursula leaves Gleiwitz

1st August 1945, 06.30hrs

Holy Mass for us. Otherwise, quiet the entire day.

2nd August 1945

I went with Vater to the Russians to negotiate about the car journey. I have little confidence in their behaviour, during the driving briefing. Vater is already going to sleep in the garage because we're supposed to leave early in the morning. I go quickly to say goodbye to the twins, get my bedroll which Gisela helps me to carry.

Frau Jendralski gives me some green cucumbers. I pack up with mother, almost the whole night, we barely sleep at all.

3rd August 1945

The car is not going today, tomorrow the journey will begin.

We are still packing up, eagerly, as there are still so many things to do. Midday in the Polish street stalls, we eat Wienersnitzel again - a good nutritional base for our forthcoming journey. In the afternoon, good old

Hampe takes our luggage, as directed, to the car garage on Bahnhof Strasse. He gets through with it, without any incident. In the evening, we go to pray for blessings, one last time, in the old chapel at the school monastery. The new Regina Pacis chapel is occupied by Russians and is shamefully used as a hospital. Then, we say goodbye to all fellow suffering refugees, the venerable nuns and to Curate Schenk. Will we be allowed to see each other one more time? They did so much good and proved to us that they had tried, with all their might, to make our trip to the German side possible. With their help, it succeeded. Please pray for us, that all goes well and that we find Christel healthy and well. We will do the same for you, Herr Curate Schenk, because we know only too well, how difficult it is for you in 'this environment'.

"Journey in God's name," are their parting words.

With some more hand luggage, we make our way to the car garage. On the way, an incident with five, armed Polish. Luckily, it goes well, and we can continue. At their bidding, we can say goodbye to Onkel Josef, Tante Elly and Jochen. They are reluctant to let us go in one respect: Will we ever find and be allowed to see each other again.

We spend the night at the garage.

4th August 1945

The journey begins at around 05.00hrs. I am incredibly frightened and unsure if we will be able to get to the German side for certain. We are sitting or lying, thirteen of us, crammed together on pieces of luggage, our noses almost touching the tarpaulin of the truck. Herr Leirich has his place with the driver. Frau Ditriech and her two children are travelling in front of us as passengers in the Russian Major's car. Our truck stank of petrol because of the three barrels we were carrying. As there was no escaping it, we ripped back the tarpaulin to let some fresh air flow in. So, at dawn, we leave our hometown - not a glorious parting, into which we have been forced. Hopefully, it will all go well and without incident - that is my constant thought, and luckily, so far, so good. In the school monastery, the venerable nuns and Curate Schenk pray for the success of our journey. Beyond Oppeln and onto Siegersdorf/Kreis Bünzlaü, we chance it past the Russians, twice. We drive past Breslau, going towards Liegnitz, where there are two Russian control points. Our fears were unfounded as it all went smoothly. We should have been driven to Löbaü-Reichenbach, but after we've already been driven a fair way in that direction, we're taken back to Görlitz because the Major must get to Vienna. So far travelled! Only to arrive together back in Görlitz, where we are accommodated in a refugee camp that is primitive and dirty.

5th August 1945

Lord's Day. Went to church at 18.00hrs. Slept so badly last night. (We meet Werner Skroch and the Volkmer family, also in Görlitz) Mutti and I find private quarters for the night, sleep well and wake refreshed.

6th August 1945

Nothing special. Write a letter to Onkel Joseph and give it for posting.

7th August 1945.

Up early at 05.00hrs and had to drive to Löbaü in the van, an extra 2km because of the bridge blast. Here, we found Frau Klimanck from Katowitz. We spend the night in a school and must be up early to go to Ebersdorf.

8th August 1945

Early morning, we continue our journey to Ebersdorf. At Pützkaü we must walk again, this time 5 km, and with our luggage! We still managed to catch the train and could travel further to Dresden. In Dresden, where the old town has been destroyed, we are assigned to a refugee camp that is so awful, we cannot stay there. Luckily, we find a place to stay for a few days with a nice family.

9th August 1945

Midday, we eat in Radebeüt. Then we drove through Dresden Old Town - organised by Vater. Frau Klimanck leaves this evening. Mutti takes her to the station. We get plums from Frau Wenk - they tasted so good.

10th August 1945

Did some washing at Frau Zeller's, then helped her. Packed up our things together, ready for tomorrow.

11th August 1945

We didn't leave after all. Helped Frau Zeller, in whose house we are living. Slept in the afternoon. Given biscuits, bread and tobacco by Frau Wenk.

12th August 1945

At 07.15hrs, in pouring rain, we're driven to the Dresden main station. The train leaves at 10.00hrs through to Glaüchaü. Here, we will get off and change trains for Gera.

This Sunday is unfortunately a day for travel, so we can't go to church.

Frau Zeller gives us a full set of cooking utensils and a good potato salad to take with us. At 21.35hrs we arrive in Gera. We are received by the DRK *(Deutsche Rötes Kreutz - German Red Cross)* and taken to our overnight accommodation. We are given something to eat, however, we don't sleep.

13th August 1945

Moved early to a small hotel. Nothing special but a wonderfully comfortable bed. Midday and evening we eat in the concert hall. Mutti and Vater get food stamps and meet Frau Güsella there.

14th August 1945

Slept until 11.00hrs! Mutti out to get food tokens. Vater in Eisenberg with Herrn Schwarz. Midday meal at the concert hall, supper at the House of Crafts.

15th August 1945

Nothing special. Went to the cinema in the afternoon with parents: - 'Das Herz müß Schweigen.' (*The Heart Must Be Silent*)

Dreamt of Wolfhart and Hannelore last night, Vater dreamt of Onkel Josef.

16th August 1945

Vater went to Schmölln (*25km east of Gera*), for finance. He was back by midday. He looks for private quarters. With Mutti for support, we go to the catholic church.

17th August 1945

Go to Mass with Mutti. The Schwarz family all go to Eisenberg today. We write to the Wahrenbrück police about Christel.

18th August 1945

At midday, moved to 67, Galgenberg Strasse in Gera, where we have a room in Frau Sperling's apartment. Parents go to town again. I stay at home.

19th August 1945

Lord's Day - Church at St Elisabeth's at 10.00hrs. At 12.00hrs we eat at the Central Cafe. Write to the vicarage in Liebenwerda to ask about Christel. Parents out in the afternoon to see what they can find around the town. I stay at home.

20th - 21st August 1945

Nothing special happened. On 21st August, I go to town with Mutti where we go to the station to get our backpacks. There we met Hilde Sicha who came from Leipzig.

22nd August 1945

Vater went early to Eisenberg. Doesn't encounter Herr Schwarz or his family. Mutti and I fetch the basket from the station - now we can make a pudding with the powder we brought back.

23rd August 1945

Got up early. Parents went to get coal first, then went across country; it was worth it.

24th August 1945

Vater went early to Weimar. Baked two apple cakes with Mutti and went to town in the afternoon. Also did some washing.

(Weimar, 72km west of Gera, was an important Nazi administration city, second only to Berlin.)

25th August 1945

Parents fetched coal. Saturday work. Parents went to look round town in the afternoon, to see if they could find anything useful.

Dreamt of the monastery today.

26th August 1945

Lord's day. Church at 08.45hrs. Met Frau Britta. Then I went with Vater to the station because we still had luggage there; and for our travel tickets. In the afternoon, parents get apples.

27th August 1945

Parents travel early to Weimar. I bake biscuits in the afternoon as I am alone.

At the DRK in Weimar they ask after whereabouts of Christel, Oma Ciba and Tante Dorchen.

28th August 1945

Nothing special. Went to Cinema[23]: Suspicion of Ursula' ('Verdacht auf Ursula') A German crime thriller from 1939 by Karl Heinz Martin, based on the novel, 'Ursula Floats By', by Walter Harich.

29th August 1945

Went with Vater to Töppeln, (*8 km west of Gera*) to collect mushrooms.

(Might I see Wolfhart ??!!!??)

30th - 31st August 1945

Nothing special happened. On 31st August Parents go to Töppeln, to collect mushrooms.

---

23 Visual arts became popular once again, since theatres and cinemas had been shut down in recent years and people enjoyed the normality of visiting the cinema. Dancing was also popular. Many dance schools opened up, sometimes even in the ruins of bombed-out buildings.

CHAPTER SIXTEEN

Sad news for Christa-Maria

Wednesday 1st August 1945. Tepl

Cold. Quick operation in the consultations today. Alone with Erika in the afternoon.

Dr. May in Tepl. Two ward visits to the barracks with Dr. May.

The May family have been so kind to us both. Frau Dr. May has something motherly about her, that is clearly felt by us. Yes, we are so grateful that Dr. May has taken us on and is teaching us things we can use in everyday life. It is a task that we pursue with joy because it suits us better than mucking out; a job which is now also behind us!

Thursday 2nd August 1945

Somewhat milder weather - still wearing my winter pants though.

Again, happy to help with the consultations. Went to visit the sick in the afternoon.

Given a few left-over peas by Frau Dr. May for lunch. In the evening everyone got a piece of chocolate from the American with the wobbly head - so good.

Wrote in my notebook this evening.

Friday 3rd August 1945

An exceedingly difficult day. News about the result of the Potsdam Conference.[24] Our home is Polish!

All Germans are to be expelled from their homeland. Where will you be, my dearest parents and Uschi? When will I ever reach you again? Until now, one has always had the hope that perhaps one would come home again. But now? I must seriously control myself, so as not to cry aloud, as we look at the map with Frau Dr. May. Even if I had no intense patriotic feeling for our Third Reich, it is now all the stronger. I am German and I want to remain German. If I didn't have my Lord God, I would fail to bear this.

Today is feast of Sacred Heart of Jesus - thereby linked to another strong memory of home.

My home! Now no longer German - Polish! Tears roll down my cheeks because of this.

My dear mother heart - perhaps the good Lord will let us meet each other again!

So difficult to read from 'Ja, Vater' today. I will say some of the prayers, at least, I will think them.

---

24 The Potsdam Conference was held between 17th July - 2nd August 1945 in Potsdam, Germany. The leaders of the allied forces made decisions about the administration of defeated Germany and post WW2 settlement. This included, among other things, (1) the division of Germany into the four zones controlled by the allied forces - Russian, United States of America, French and British. (2) The transfer of German territories east of the Oder/Neisse line to Poland and the Soviet Union. (3) The demilitarisation and denazification of Germany to eliminate the threat of war and remove Nazi ideology and influence.

Frau Dr. May is touchingly kind to us. She must also suffer because of this Potsdam announcement.

Each helps the other to lighten their heavy load a little.

Lord God! Help us all.

There is no shortage of joy on this day either. A good pea soup for lunch. In the afternoon, an orange and a piece of chocolate for each of us from an American. We gave our oranges to Dr. May's two boys. We shared in their immense joy a little, as we saw their happy faces.

This evening we have potato soup with Tante Mia. She brought potatoes from Tepl yesterday.

We only have potato flakes and a few peas. God, take care of us - Amen.

Saturday 4th August 1945

A day with much joy. The good Lord has again sent us warm rays of sunshine.

Frau Dr. May is so motherly to us. Something emanates from her that makes us feel so good. As soon as she said, "I am obliged to take care of you. I wouldn't even know how to behave in front of your parents if I did not." I'm so grateful, I can't find the words. Because where you feel the most, you don't have to say much.

Frau Dr. May got us a cup of warm milk and a left over, half slice of cornbread before the afternoon consulting session - our joy was indescribable. I just had to think: God won't leave you after all.

We received kartoffelpuffer (*potato cakes*) from Tante Mia in the afternoon. That wasn't all we received that afternoon - from Frau Dr. May we got a piece of mohnkuchen (*poppyseed cake*) and a cup of coffee. In the poppyseed, some dried grated orange peel had been added so we simply had to taste it! After supper, we went to Frau Dr. May and were allowed to iron our blouses and uniforms. It was wonderfully comfortable there and Uncle Doctor told us about his school and time as a student.

I had longed so much for people, for those with whom one could always feel a connection without speaking much, and with whom one could talk 'from soul to soul'. Frau Dr. May is one such person. Perhaps I will write more about this woman, who will always be dear to me.

Sunday 5th August 1945

Lord's Day.

Sadly, I couldn't go to church service today. Erika was at Holy Mass today and, as there were patients with various ailments to see to, it was my turn to stay behind and cook on the wagon, as Erika had done the Sunday before last.

I felt rather good in the doctor's short sleeved white coat; I no longer looked like a nurse but more like a receptionist. Mutti and Vater and Ursula! If you could see me like this! All three of you would be incredibly pleased with your youngest - take pleasure there! You worry about me unnecessarily. Perhaps we will quickly find each other somewhere in the Reich since you have also had to leave your home. God will pour everything in to make this happen.

Monday 6th August 1945

Washed laundry in the lunch break. Frau Dr. May let us wash our nurses' aprons and starch them. I ironed them in the evening, along with my other clean washing. Got another 'hit' in the kitchen this evening. A beautiful warm day.

Tuesday 7th August 1945

Before consultations, I went with Dr. May to see the Major, the camp commander, to talk about the state of health in the camp. I interpreted.

I, who sometimes believe I'm not good for anything other than spreading muck on a field, can slowly but surely, and modestly, begin to believe in myself. I only want to be what I am, if only I knew what that was.

In the morning, had a bit more teaching. We spoke about leg swellings and ulcers.

Wednesday 8th August 1945

It is already dark outside. A long day of demanding work lies behind me.

We were down in the consulting room until 20.30hrs. The wringing out of the washed bandages was such arduous work, but we were happy in our work, because it had poured with rain all day and we were thankful to have a proper roof over our heads. In the afternoon Frau Dr. May gave us a slice of bread with raspberry jam and a cup of coffee. She really 'mothers' us!

In the afternoon, I ate the two pieces of chocolate the Americans had given us yesterday.

Unfortunately, the day was overshadowed by the terrible noise again at the front of the Trek.

It hurts me terribly, how in these challenging times, people make their already hard life, hell, through eternal quarrels. Instead of love, through which they could forgive, forget and bring sunshine to these dark days, they choose to be so stubborn and bitter. It is so hard to judge one and agree with the other. I don't want to hurt anyone. God! Let us become one united flock.

The camp hospital was opened today.

My dearest parents and you, my dear sister, I send greetings at the end of the day. Our dear God is looking after me in the most wonderful of ways. Don't worry about your youngest.

Thursday 9th August 1945

Everything is happening early this morning; the whole camp is supposed to start moving home tomorrow morning. But it's 20.00hrs and they're saying that we won't move until Saturday.

Today, on the alleged last day, was of course terribly busy. Everyone wanted to have a travel bandage put on. We also had work enough, stowing away the medicaments that we had to take with us. Our hospital in the camp is just being finished. It really looks nice.

Today, very cold and wet. They say that this former RAD Camp we are in now, is to be a prisoner of war camp run by the Czechs. The thought of this makes one cold. The poor Germans!

It's supposed to be about going home! One can't believe it yet!

See you again soon, my beloved ones; it's all happening so quickly, it's almost too difficult to understand. But be happy with me about us meeting again soon.

Friday 10th August 1945

It poured with rain all day. The water soaked through wagons, all standing ready to leave. It is desolate in this cruel weather! The mood of the people has fallen a lot due to this external uneasiness. The storm is so bad that the trees in the forest topple like matchsticks. Therefore, the horses must be brought out from the forest. People and animals are really being plagued today. And to add to this, the major's icy cold, irritated and angry face. And we two nurses were allowed to sit by the stove in our much loved, lived in, consulting room to keep warm. You don't want to venture out in this relentlessly wet place!

I will not forget the ambulance that went to Marienbad today. In all haste, they climb in and say a brief goodbye; then off the ambulance goes.

But what may have happened to these individuals that no one sees or senses?

There, a mother was led to give birth. She had distributed her other children among the people, who took care of them. She went to the Czech town of Marienbad to give life to her child. How might this woman have felt on the inside?

Herr Ernst went with them to say goodbye to his wife who was buried in Marienbad last Saturday, so far from home and in a foreign country. There was certainly a lot going on inside him which he probably tried to suppress.

An old mother is also carried away, too weak to travel; away from her loved ones, without knowing when she will be capable of travel or when she will see them again.

Another woman asked me to tell the ambulance driver to wait. She wanted the birth certificate for her eleven-day old baby from the hospital nurse, if she would let her have it. The woman had no Czech money and therefore couldn't pay for a birth certificate in Marienbad. Now, she has this eleven-day old little baby, wrapped like a caterpillar in a cocoon, and wants to come on the Trek in all kinds of wind and weather!

So, each one has their own troubles to carry, each one a silent hero.

For supper, dry bread, nothing else. Earlier, I had eaten a canteen of thin, burnt gruel and a cold, stale dry piece of bread. Peas for lunch and two slices of dry toast in the evening.

Frau Dr. May was once again very motherly to us. She helped us finish wrapping the Red Cross bandages and repaired our blankets, inherited from RAD Wahrenbrück, and sleeping bags with her own thread.

She sewed the number 15, my number from the work service, on my blanket bag so it would be identifiable. In the evening she helped us into our sleeping bags and gave us both some warm Russian tea. We were really embarrassed.

Saturday 11th August 1945. Leaving Tepl

Woken early by Frau Dr. May. No sooner were we out of bed than we were brought breakfast. At 08.00hrs, we set off. The major thanked us both very nicely. He gave us boiled sweets and chewing gum, his manner was very personable.

Until Theüsing, I travelled in the American's car. First with Dixon and a medical student; then further with a Lieutenant - he stuck a piece of orange in our mouths and gave us a cream candy.

In Theüsing, a woman gives me a bowl of soup with cooked rabbit in it and a slice of bread. There are only Russians and Czechs here. Until now, only the Americans have been with us. Having been treated kindly by the Americans, it wasn't easy to get used to these completely different people.

We can no longer start a conversation with our English. There were great rumours going round about being transported to Siberia and so on.

It rained in the afternoon. We had no shelter.

Wandered around until it got dark, then slept on the Dehmelt's wagon.

Sunday 12th August 1945

I have never yet lived through such a strange Sunday!

At 05.30hrs, without any breakfast, we were marched off! Got very wet. Czech and Russians had plundered a lot during the night. Watches, bicycles, rubber laundry boots.

High mountains had to be overcome, they ran continuously. In Büchau, we received a cup of coffee.

Late in the afternoon, hiked along the river Eger between the towering mountains. Unfortunately, one wasn't so in awe because of being overtired. Came through Bad Gishübel. Here the river Eger overflowed. We stood on the country road, waiting in the dark. During our Sunday 'tour' have seen remnants of war in the ditches - bazookas, hand grenades, shot up cars and so on.

Monday and Tuesday 13th - 14th August 1945

Stood on the country road for two days. The Czechs marched up and down with their rifles on show, over their shoulders. After two days we got something warm to eat again. Treated a few sick people. Slept overnight on Frau Siedel's wagon. The first night was very miserable on the cart - the weather was changeable and when it was raining and windy there was no shelter.

Wednesday 15th August 1945. Feast of the Assumption

Prepared for departure to Neudorf train station. We're only allowed to take hand luggage we can carry ourselves. Horses, wagons and all left over luggage must stay here.

The day before, the men had made ramps for the wagons to be loaded. Everyone was of the firm belief that they could bring their things with them. The indignation was bad!

As we travelled to the station, the roadside ditches were a terrible picture - a pot, a smoking oven, lunch still in the pot, possessions, clothes and shoes, all in the ditch. I found fried potatoes on a stove behind a wagon which I greedily devoured. It was evening before everything was loaded.

It wasn't so bad for the two of us, Erika and me. Since we are carrying all our things anyway, we could take them with us. It was exceedingly difficult for those who got on the open feed train trucks, with only their hand luggage. Had to leave the horses and loaded carts behind for the Czechs. It all happened so quickly that the people hardly knew what was happening.

This Wednesday we inherited some clothes from Frau Dr. May, and I got a dress from Frau Kulozik. Erika and I had half a bread roll each.

Thursday 16th August 1945

Survived the night in the open feed train truck. It rained but only my blanket got wet, not me.

Now we've been standing for three hours in Teplitz-Schönaü. There are no German signs to read, only Czech. One hears only Czech. People slouch over their luggage, some asleep, some chewing, children crying. This unfamiliar environment is so strange and uncomfortable.

Where the train is going, no-one knows. One hopes to Silesia!

Ah, my dear mother heart, if only I could be with you soon.

Friday 17th August 1945, written on Tuesday 21st August 1945

Dreamt of Dr. May. Frau Dr. May had tears in her eyes when I told her.

After we had waited in Teplitz-Schönau for 8.5 hours, in the grey light of dawn, after a scary night journey, we arrived at a camp. Barbed wire all around us, former concentration camp people with their rifles on show, everything dirty. Louse-riddled Russians had lived in it. Herr Kulozik died on this dark night. During the day, each person quickly prepared something for themselves to eat. Czechs were standing everywhere with their whips and rubber truncheons. Some young Sudetenland Germans, who had also been expelled from their homeland, were among this group of miserable refugees.

Saturday 18th August 1945

Seestadel is the name of this place here, between Brüse and Komotaü.

Today, we set off early, with 30kg of luggage. The number of peoples' good things that had to be left behind in the barracks is indescribable. All these things, taken from people who will come home as beggars and find nothing. If the camp was thrown open, the Czech's luggage would be ransacked. The 'brothers' had already eyed up the gold and silver objects, fabrics, new pieces of clothing and groceries, especially bacon. It was hard to believe the number of pieces of bacon that suddenly turned up and were quickly distributed before the checkpoint.

I've also been getting nerves in my stomach for weeks. Before it was my turn to be checked, I quickly tore up both my Hitler Youth identity cards and threw my climbing vest[25] from my suitcase. Apart from my fountain pen, small brown propelling pencil and the case, nothing was taken from me. I only noticed later that these things were missing, so cleverly did the guy steal them.

Therefore, I am writing in pencil!

My wallet, that had the Bund Deutsche Mädchen (League of German Girls) identity cards in, was checked for gold crowns[26].

Slept until late afternoon, lying between the railway tracks. We were given nothing to eat.

Waited in vain for the transport all day. Then ordered back to the camp.

In the evening we made pancakes from the flour, water and sugar a woman gave us. From the kitchen we got some flour soup. I washed in the evening. The whole area seems unsafe. Later, I heard gunshots close by.

Sunday 19th August 1945

I have not lived through such a strange Sunday as this before. In all haste and hurry, packed up ready and waited for the trek to head off again. We must go towards the border in trucks. Waited and waited the entire day. I couldn't get my backpack onto the already crammed truck. I tried to

---

25 A climbing vest is a lightweight jacket with external pockets for carrying maps, ropes, compass and flasks for outdoor activities. Refugees were subjected to strict border controls and identity checks. Possession of a climbing vest raised suspicion of being a spy, collaborator or carrying weapons and contraband. By getting rid of her vest, Christa-Maria was without a useful item for carrying things and keeping her warm. She must have thought it worth the risk, to avoid being seen as suspicious by border guards and other refugees.

26 Gold crowns refers to dental crowns rather than money. Due to malnourishment, gold crown often came loose and were kept hidden in a secret place. The discovery of a gold crown by border guards meant a refugee's nationality could be identified and prove their eligibility status for financial help i.e. if you could afford gold crowns you didn't need any aid.

practice my Sunday observance that day; I sang my song to the Lord, but I couldn't be satisfied.

On Sunday evening we were in a different barracks. A bit friendlier and more comfortable than before. Full body wash and hair wash in the evening.

Monday 20th August 1945

Again, we waited in the yard till afternoon, leaned on the pieces of luggage, because again, we could not get going. Cooked a great soup with mushrooms, there was also a pot of sago, other stuff we found and then also some flour. In the morning I read some 'Wandrer', [27]which I have in addition to letters from home and 'Ja Vater' book that I found by chance yesterday in the washroom – stuck it in the front of my dress. The first few pages made me feel so many beautiful, important things which I did not realise when I had read it at home; where one did not have to worry, where one had everything. Now, from the trenches, one understands far better what was written.

I was and am, considering the circumstances, quite satisfied.

I just say "Ja, Vater" and there it goes again, my soul is lifted.

Socks and tights washed in the evening.

Tuesday 21st August 1945

Absolutely no trucks going anywhere. We must stay here again today. At 16.oohrs we had pea soup. Whether we have reached the low point here in this camp, or whether it will still go further downhill, one can't say.

---

27 'Wandrer' known as 'Thus Spoke Zarathustra' in English was written by philosopher Frederich Nietzsche and explores his views on humanity, morality and the meaning of life.

My old fountain pen broke today. That made me feel sad. I have such longing for home today.

I read two letters from Uschi today - her birthday letter and the Christmas one. Both tell me, quite reassuringly, of your love for me, my Uschilein.

Wednesday 22nd August 1945. Deutscheinsiedel.[28]

Quite unexpectedly, buses were there this morning. We hurried to get ready. I could only take my handbag and RAD blanket wrapped around my shoulders. Hopefully, the rest of the luggage will follow on in the truck. We had a wonderful journey until we arrived at the border - looming mountains, small practical allotment gardens, trees richly laden with ripe fruit and mountain streams. One could be happy about that. It was painful to see nothing German here, just Czech and Russian flags, in the windows, pictures of Czech and Russian statesmen. No German words, only Czech blaring out all around me. Yesterday, German land; today, Czech land. All signs and directions only in Czech. It will be like this at home too, everything in Polish.

Arrived at the barrier; men, women and children must stand separately to be counted. Walked 12km to Sayda with hand luggage. Got soaked on the way. Received warmly in Sayda, found reasonable accommodation in a small guest house. Had three slices of bread, a dollop of jam and some hot coffee to drink. For doing the washing up, I received a plate of flour soup. There is a piano in the next room. Erika played a few Mozart pieces that brought back fond memories and I played some old tunes that I used to play on our lovely piano in the dining room at home. A ray of sunshine had broken through the gloomy day.

---

28 Deutscheinsiedel is a small town on the German/ Czech Republic border where Christa-Maria crossed back into Germany from what was then Czechoslovakia.

Thursday 23rd August 1945

Early in the morning we travelled on a passenger train to Freiberg/Sa. (*A town in Saxony, 30 km north of the Czech Republic border.*)

Got off train in Mülda. Station destroyed. You couldn't get into the stinking concourse at the station. We were given two days' worth of food vouchers. Now, in Germany, the refugees are left to their own devices and must feed themselves from their own pockets. There is also another concern - the question of money. There's no such thing as a post office savings book.

In Freiberg, one sees so many fine and decent people. And I, I look like some sort of tramp. One ruins the few things one has, terribly.

I, Christa Ciba must look at all this for myself. I am so ashamed to have stumbled into ruin. Crouched and wept at the edge of a green area this morning, because now everyone is left to their own devices and can go where they want. There I crouched, hungry on the street and didn't know where to go.

Decided to push forward, going from station to station with the others.

Bought 30g of salami with the food tokens - haven't had that in a long, long time. Wasn't given any lunch. The baker gave me invalid 5 RM (Reichsmark) tokens in change, so I went back there in the afternoon, but it was all in vain, and in all my layers, I was quite hot.

Travelled to Nossen in the afternoon.

There we gathered windfall apples from under a tree.

Had a warm potato to eat in the evening. Overnight in a smelly station waiting room behind the counter, to sleep.

Friday 24th August 1945

A warm cup of tea from Frau Hesse this morning.

We travelled from Nossen to Riesa.

For lunch, used some food token to get 50g Eiergraupen[29] to eat. Then I went to town by myself and bought carrots. What did I look like in my winter coat and track suit bottoms, in a heat wave?

I passed by so many nicely dressed people, but I couldn't look at them.

The train to Leipzig leaves with three hours delay. I'm so overwhelmed. It's impossible to get ahead. Slept in a tunnel on the floor.

Saturday 25th August 1945

I woke up to realise my suitcase had been stolen. I should have put it by Mia's side, who was lying on the outside, so that it couldn't be seen. And in the morning, it was gone. I looked around the station, but it was nowhere to be seen. Travelled from Riesa to Döbeln in a bomb-shelled train. We hadn't bought tickets, rather used our refugee travel documents. Arrived in Leipzig at noon - the mighty terminus pretty much destroyed. Got into a Red Cross barracks after a long wait. Received pea soup as the day's ration of food. Had to pay 0.40 RM for it. One just wasn't full. We didn't have any more bread. In my suitcase, I still had some apples and carrots. On top of all the misery, the loss of the suitcase! But I didn't worry about it too much, because I see our poor soldiers, emaciated and in rags, bearded, with only an empty bread bag hanging on them. Their big questioning eyes, facing the desolation - homeless, destitute and left to themselves, seen with melancholy. Then every complaint will be silenced

---

29 Eiergraupen is a traditional eastern German dish made from chopped hard-boiled eggs and semolina. During wartime shortages, the semolina porridge was made with water and a little salt, if available.

because these poor young people have already lived under great hardship for six years and now.... now such a high price to pay in the end. I hardly felt any war hardship during those years whilst in Gleiwitz. Even if our future is a vague question mark, we continue with courage and trust in God. In Leipzig, I saw lots of young people marked with the Soviet star: Communist Party of Deutschland. (KPD) My Fatherland will now be ruled by this party. No German officers, for whom I kept an eye open, do I see anymore. Ach! my Germany, how changed do I find you now? Received some vegetable stew and a bread roll from Tante Mia. I make a special note of that because it is truly remarkable for her to share. In the late afternoon, travelled to Halle in an open cattle feed wagon. A different Saturday afternoon! In Halle, one also saw the destruction through bombing. Spent the night at the train station, stretched out on the cold stone floor.

Sunday 26th August 1945, Lord's Day

Got on the train to Aschersleben this morning, which was deployed from Halle incredibly early. I managed to get a nice window seat this time. Here, I read letters and my book 'Wandrer.' I really got something from it for this Sunday. A glorious day, created for the glory of God.

As travelling companions, two old ladies from Prague, a youthful lady and her son, a doctor. They had lost everything; a gorgeous villa and everything that belonged to their wealthy lifestyle. This woman had only 4RM in her purse because the Czechs had taken all her crowns away. When I heard this, I thought, yes, now I am rich, still with my 40 RM. In Halle, Paul Hentschol, left us to find his relatives. We arrived in Aschersleben at noon. At 15.30hrs received some semolina soup, without any money. Again, no bread the entire day. Then travelled on to

Quedlinburg. Although I was desperately looking, I didn't see anyone I knew on the way.

Hungry, Hungry, Hungry.

God, look after us. Little girl brought us both potato soup and a little piece of bread. Slept in the waiting room under the counter.

Monday 27th August 1945

Went begging in the morning. At the first house, the door was opened by a Russian soldier! Imagine our fright - what would he do with us? would we be shot? - faced with this man in a Russian uniform, occupying a civilian house! But he was quite pleasant, invited us into the kitchen and gave us a slice of bread each with some jam! In the bakery, three bread rolls each. In another house, some apples and windfall pears. Bought 50g semolina with the two-day food tokens and was given 100g. At another bakers, used the tokens to buy 600g of bread. That's how one makes one's way through Quedlinburg - a quaint, old town with a rich and preserved history. It is so friendly. Here, one can really feel something of peace. The old gabled houses on the market square and on the narrow streets takes one back to the Middle Ages. Begged for potatoes in the afternoon. Got some carrots from Frau Dehmelt. Cooked carrot stew for supper - it tasted wonderful.

Tuesday, 28th August 1945, written on Sunday, September 2nd, 1945

Sat in the railway station in Quedlinburg. In the afternoon, a man came to us who wanted a girl to work on a farm near Ditfürt. With the permission of the Trek supervisor, Herr Ernst, Erika and I travelled at 19.00hrs to Ditfürt, to the Drilling family. There, we were given supper. Then, Herr and Frau Kramm came to get a young girl to work on their farm. They came to see the maid, to look me up and down, that's how I felt. But what can you do in order not to starve and to eke out an existence for the time being. Of course, one would only arrive with hesitation since one isn't a specialist and neither of us know anything about farming. We both slept at the Drillings.

One thinks about this, what it means for us: we are being asked to go and work for the farmers. One takes it all in - to finally have a place to stay and not ruin oneself, slouched in a ditch.

Wednesday 29th August 1945

Up early at 07.00hrs. Herr Kramm comes to wake me.

Chopped turnips for the cows, then spent entire day on the potato field. Had food to eat. Frau Kramm had prepared a lunch basket for me to take to the field. Wasn't hungry! The people were nice to me. I should make myself at home.

Thursday 30th August 1945

Same work as yesterday in a heatwave. Have a modest little room just for me - my dearest wish. A bed of my own after such a long time, a bed already so precious to me. Now, in the great famine, I get such decent food. God really cares for me. I sing a song of thanksgiving to the Lord.

Friday 31st August 1945

Again, entire day in the field. Did laundry in the evening.
Child tired.

CHAPTER SEVENTEEN

Ursula searches for news of Christa-Maria

1st September 1945

Saturday work - Baked biscuits.

2nd September 1945

Lord's Day. Church at 08. 45hrs. Then went with Vater to the train station to exchange money. Went to town in the afternoon. Visited hospital and Dürrenebersdorf. Gleiwitzer people lay there. But not Christel. Then coffee at home.

3rd September 1945

Hilde Sicha and 'Peggi' here. I had just washed my hair, then went to the employment office - temporarily not operational. Handed in my letters for Onkel Josef and the monastery - they should go by Wednesday.

4ᵗʰ - 5ᵗʰ September 1945

Nothing special. 5ᵗʰ September - went back to the hospital, to Sister Maria Klausberg. Met some people from Gleiwitz – no-one has any news of Christel. Was given bread, potatoes and apples.

Hilda Sicha here.

6ᵗʰ September 1945

In Kraftsdorf, 11km West of Gera, with Frau Sperling, to get mushrooms. Not a good harvest but found more blackberries than usual. Met people from Gleiwitz on the train. Hilde at our flat - she leaves Peggi with us because she must go to Leipzig.

7ᵗʰ September 1945

Sacred Heart Friday. After Mass went to the agency on Harbon Strasse to see if there was any news of Christel but there was nothing. In the afternoon I went into town with Peggi

8ᵗʰ September 1945

Saturday work. Baked cakes and ironed. Parents in the town. Gave in post to the west. Expect reply 25ᵗʰ September 1945.

9ᵗʰ September 1945

Lord's Day. Church at 08.45hrs. Went to confession. Hilde was with us for lunch, afternoon coffee and supper. After lunch, went to the Otto von Bismarck Memorial Tower in Northeastern area of Gera. Vater met Gladisch, the wood merchant who drove to Mühlhausen, 150km West of Gera.

10th September 1945

Was with Mutti at Hilda's late afternoon where we had good cakes and biscuits.

11th - 12th September 1945

Nothing special - 11th September went to get wood from Hilde.

13th September 1945

Afternoon in town, looking. Went to hospital but achieve nothing. No news of Christel. Met parents in town.

14th September 1945

Travelled early on train to Leipzig - there was a buffet car!! Visited the Monument to Battle of Nations and the Zoo. Went home alone in the evening as Hilde was staying over Sunday night at her sister, Mieze's.

15th September 1945

Mutti stacking potatoes in the afternoon; I go with Vater to town to look for groceries.

16th September 1945

Lord's Day. Church at 08.45hrs. Meet two people from Gleiwitz - the Pawlik Family from the Marien Lyceum, whom I visit in the afternoon. They're going to Munich.

17th September 1945

Parents go early to Eisenberg; they bring back bread. From the Schwarz family, whom they met today, they hear that Dr. Oles and his wife are in Weissenfels.

18th September 1945

Mutti stacks potatoes. We go to Töppeln to get blackberries and some potatoes. Hilde here. Vater must go to Leipzig on Friday.

19th September 1945

Made marmalade, stacked wood, separated potatoes.

In the evening, parents went to see the people from Breslau who are going to the West.

20th September 1945

Mutti stacks potatoes in the afternoon. Hilde is here. I went to the town hospital.

Was given some bread.

21st September 1945

Vater in Leipzig at Mieze's about the border crossing to Bavaria. Is given tinned meat for the journey. Pick Vater up from the station.

22nd September 1945

Saturday works. Yeast and poppyseed rolls baked. Get groceries in the afternoon. Hilde in Wünchendorf.

23ʳᵈ September 1945

Lord's Day. Church at 08.45hrs (clocks set back one hour) Spoke to nice Rheinlander about the border crossing. Tinned meat and green dumplings for lunch. Hilde came after coffee and stayed for supper.

24ᵗʰ September 1945

About 08.00hrs Vater went to Saalfeld, to sort out about getting across the inner German border from East Germany to the West German side. I go with Mutti to church and into town. Ask at the Schlesinger Leatherware factory about working from home.

Hilde here - Peggi has been sold.

25ᵗʰ September 1945

Went with Mutti early evening to the train station, where we met some people from Gleiwitz, who, with the Walde's and Fraulein Pruschowska, drove together to Bautzen.

26ᵗʰ September 1945

I go early to Wünchendorf with Hilde. We walk to Endschütz. I bring twenty apples.

27ᵗʰ September 1945

Nothing special. Could not go to the hospital because it was raining so much.

28th September 1945

Nothing special.

29th September 1945

Saturday work. Baked poppyseed rolls. Went to train station at midday, thinking I was to meet Vater, but he wasn't there.

At 19.00hrs, Michaelmas celebration.

30th September 1945

Lord's Day. Church at 08.45hrs. Hilde came for lunch. In the afternoon I go with Hilde to the Dyers Tower. We get some vegetables there. Vater still not back from Saalfeld yet.

CHAPTER EIGHTEEN

Christa-Maria in Ditfürt

Saturday 1ˢᵗ September 1945. Ditfürt

Brought home 23 sacks of potatoes again.

Very cold.

In the evening, ironing and mending.

Sunday 2ⁿᵈ September 1945. Ditfürt

Incredibly sad that today, on The Lord's Day, I must do scouring, sweeping and servile work until midday without going to Church. Such a Sunday I have never experienced. But I opened my mouth, spoke up and let my opinion shine through. In any case, it hurt me a lot that I couldn't give my Lord God his due honour on this day. Well, I would see if I could change that! But I can arrange Sundays as I want, even though there is no substitute for attending Holy Mass. Despite my working, Sunday is different from the other days of the week and that satisfies me somewhat, if not completely.

Muttilein, Vatele, und Uschile, I am well. I must work ridiculously hard, but our dear God helps me. Every day I send up my prayer in the hope that we will find each other again. May God be never far from you in your difficult and weak hours. Mother's heart - don't bear your burden of sorrow too heavily; it has been brought home to us through God's wise counsel.

With warmest love and heartfelt gratitude, I am, as always, your Youngest.

(Now a maid.)

Sunday 9th September 1945

Went to church. Homesick.

Wednesday 12th September 1945

I sit in my room by the faint candlelight and continue my diary, shadows flickering on the walls.

In the evenings, I always allow myself a few minutes, in complete silence, forgetting the arduous work of the day. Being at peace with oneself and letting the never to be repeated day pass by with its joys and sorrows.

I truly have plenty of joys. I believe that even though the here and now looks so dark and cheerless, there is still so much beauty that just needs to be seen. One mustn't shut oneself off from the joy. All day long, I can bathe in the rich, warm autumn air, looking at God's beautiful nature; the widespread carpets of fertile fields, either already cleared and dug in earthy brown or the juicy green turnip fields next to the dry yellow bean areas. The view stretches far, far to the horizon, where heaven unites with earth, unless interrupted by the rising, dense clouds of smoke from the burning potato leaf fires.

I am full of thanks and joy, when I see how the richly blessed autumn fruits of the fields can help lift my spirits.

Despite the many injustices in the world, God allows the fruits of the earth to thrive, whether humanity deserves his goodness or not.

A full basket of potatoes is true bliss today - when thousands are starving, they would have given us a lot to get their hands on this full basket.

The work is hard - it's not easy for me but always gives me an overall feeling of warmth and sunny rays of joy break through to illuminate the darkness.

I could still write much more about the pleasant things that I am probably, consciously looking for everywhere, but then it would be too long winded.

I am tired and my candle gets lower.

Thank you, dear God for the day today.

Friday 14ᵗʰ September 1945
Threshing. Full again, no longer hungry every day now. Rained in the evening. Early to bed.

Sunday 16ᵗʰ September 1945
Went to Holy Mass. Had to fight for it. Got up early and fed the animals alone.

Good spiritual sermon about the meaning of suffering; the moral and the physical sorrow.

Didn't need to scrub up as had only done light work because the boss was in the field. Herr Kramm doesn't even let me rest on the Lord's Day.

Sunday 23rd September 1945

Didn't get to church, because the two Evangelical people, Mira and Herbert, went today.

After lunch, I made my Sunday devotions in my room.

In the previous week, I received a letter from Laücha: Tante Dorchen left the day before my letter arrived. In the evening I read the holiday edition from Christmas.

My most warmly loved Parents and Sisterlein - may God be near you. You don't have to worry about me. Know that God is looking after me.

Sunday 30th September 1945. Harvest Thanksgiving

Went to church in the morning. Pastoral letter from the Bishops of Germany. Heard from the grave of St Boniface in Fülda, that our Cardinal Bertram lives no more. Our Archbishop, my strong guide! When I heard this, the tears came; and with what was written in the Pastoral Letter which resonated with me, my eyes would not dry.

We rejoice with the church that she has her freedom again.

Homesick again when I think about our lovely Sundays at home. And will we ever have those days again? Today, I'm also thinking, with gratefulness and sadness, about our own good Curate Schenk. On 28th September was his name day and birthday. What I am now, I am, in large part, because of him. Will I meet again with the ones who were just so close to me? Even when the spirit does not let itself be forced into limits and one can always be with loved ones in thought, we are too human not to have our hours of weakness.

This past week has brought back so many doubts; I may be torturing myself unnecessarily because I am thinking and brooding too much. Hopefully, I will soon see more clearly. Truth, let me know you fully.

Thanksgiving! We thank you, great mighty God, for the fruits that you allowed to grow, and commemorate your goodness and love. Thank you for not letting me go hungry now when thousands do suffer with hunger. Put an end to this misery and have mercy on your people.

Invited to a Thanksgiving celebration by the mayor. I received my first money, 25 RM (Reichsmark) and another 3RM for the work I did with the threshing machine. With my tutoring hours, the money is earned more easily. My dearest parents, you wouldn't recognise me as a maid, the way I never shy away from any work.

My God, let us find ourselves together again.

CHAPTER NINETEEN

Ursula's life in Gera

1st October 1945

Nothing special. I go with Mutti to get some cabbage in the afternoon. By the time we get home, Vater is back from Saalfeld, thank God. He has much to tell us.

2nd October 1945

Vater travels early to Leipzig to see Mieze Sicha, to report to her from Bavaria, since he did business for her there. Hilde here again this morning - obviously! We clean rose hips that Vater brought.

3rd October 1945

In the afternoon I go to find Sister Maria, who wants to go to Klausberg. The parents are on the lookout in town. Vater goes to the cinema again.

4th October 1945

Backed a few biscuits. Mutti has washing to do so I use the fire right away. Hilde is here again around midday.

5th October 1945

I finish baking the remaining biscuits. Hilde comes again, incredibly early. Apparently, she doesn't understand at all, or just doesn't want to understand, that sometimes, we just like to be alone. One or two visits are quite inappropriate because we can't get anything done in between her visits. With her background, however, she is pursuing something else!!!

6th October 1945

Saturday work. Must go with Mutti for Typhoid test. Then we get some supplies in town.

7th October 1945

Lord's Day. Church at 08.45hrs. Then cooked meat ingredients with Hilde. She still has tins of meat, which we open because the non-working people get neither fat nor meat to share. After we have eaten lunch together, we drink coffee, there is white bread and cherry jam. In the evening we are alone.

8th October 1945

Nothing special. Went to the Schlessiger Leather Factory - no jobs available for home working.

9th October 1945

Went early, with Vater, to the employment office to register. Get registration card and must return in fourteen days.

10th October 1945

Vater travels early, with Riedel, to Leipzig by car. Go with Mutti to the forest garden and Dürenebersdorf, where we beg for carrots and apples. A truck takes us a whole stretch of the way and we are given some potatoes as a gift.

11th October 1945

Hilde with us for lunch. We wait for Vater, who luckily comes at about 17.00hrs. He had missed Reidel for a lift back.

12th October 1945

Vater goes early to Oertel[30], for the Sicha family and comes back with 'rich booty'. Hilde here.

13th October 1945

Vater with Hilde in Wünschendorf. Comes back with 'booty'. Saturday work, bake cakes.

14th October 1945

Lord's day. Went to church at 07.30hrs. Hilde here for coffee - we had Mohnkuchen! Then we went together to say the rosary.

---

30 Oertel refers to the crystal glass manufacturing company founded by Hans Oertel. It was renowned for the exquisite craftsmanship and attention to detail of its glasses, vases, bowls and decorative figurines.

15th October 1945

Vater went early to Eisenberg for the Sicha's. He brings bread back with him and something from Lindner's. Went with Mutti to Frau Uhlich.

16th October 1945

Nothing special. Hilde comes early and .... thinks she's very ingenious. (Feels 'sausage' lying between the windows.) [31]

17th October 1945

Hilda moves to our apartment building. I help her.

18th October 1945

Vater meets Fraulein Proske from Eichendorff Oberschüle, Gleiwitz. We hear from her that the Jendralski's were still in Gleiwitz on 2nd September.

19th October 1945

Vater goes for a 'tour' around Gera with Hilde. They have all sorts of success and come back with booty. I went early to the basement refugee school and heard of Tante Liesel, Dr. Klüber and all things Gleiwitzer. Fraulein Witte from the town chemist reports that Oma Ciba is said to be in Neustadt.

---

31 I think this 'sausage' refers to the practice of rolling bank notes in newspaper or cloth and stuffing it between gaps in the windows as a draft excluder, hiding money from thieves and looters.

20th October 1945

Saturday Work - bedding is hung out, we have a bath and wash our hair. Then we laid down cabbage with salt, to make sauerkraut.

21st October 1945

Lord's Day. Church at 07.30hrs. Tinned meat opened, and green dumplings made. Hilde is here for lunch. For afternoon coffee, we are invited to Hilde's new flat. I eagerly knit Vater's gloves. We have supper of beetroot and fried potatoes at our flat. Heavenly!!!

22nd October 1945

Vater goes early to the ration card office. Mutti can buy wool and material. Vater meets Herrn Weigmann, who tells him the Jendralski family are no longer in Gleiwitz; they had to leave. In the afternoon, I sew with Mutti at Hilde's. We have supper together - sausage stuffing, sauerkraut and fried potatoes.

23rd October 1945

I go early to Gera train station where I meet many people from Gleiwitz; in particular, Dorle Michel. She tells me of Curate Schenk and gives me an address where I can send post to him. Report to the labour office.

24th October 1945

Luckily, Mutti gets her altered winter coat back today. It is already very cold. I write to VOH[32] Quedlinburg.

25th October 1945

Borders for postal traffic are open. I write at once to the West.

26th October 1945

Vater went with Hilde to Langenberg. (*Langenberg is a town 50km east of Gera.*)

Came back with reasonable 'booty'. We get our winter potatoes today.

27th October 1945

Saturday work. Hanneborn, the honorary mail carrier from 8th September is with us today; he has his excuses for not bringing the mail. The case, it seems, is over for us.

28th October 1945

Lord's Day. 07.30hrs to church with Mutti. At 09.00hrs Hilde is already picking up Vater to go to church - I don't understand her behaviour, coming so early. We have dumplings and mutton for lunch. No rest after lunch, Hilde is crashing around in the kitchen, with a can of sour cherries, making a pudding. I have already prepared one for us all! 16.30hrs Christ the King devotions.

---

32 VOH Vereinigte Ostdeursch Hilfsdienste, United East German Aid Services, which was a German refugee organisation helping those fleeing and displaced by WW2. There were branches throughout Germany, including Quedlinburg.

29th October 1945

At 15.45hrs we go to the cinema to see ' Gasparone.' [33] Hilde here for supper.

30th - 31st October 1945

Nothing special. 31st October around 13.00hrs I went with Vater to Rosen for Apples. On my return, naturally, Hilde is again sitting there.

---

33 Gasparone. A 1937 musical comedy in which the prefect of the town wants his son to marry a rich countess, but he is in love with a dancer, and the countess falls in love with a mysterious stranger. Directed by Georg Jacoby. Starring Marina Rökk and Leo Slezak.

CHAPTER TWENTY

Christa-Maria longs for home

Sunday 7th October 1945. Feast of Holy Rosary

Went to Holy Mass this morning. One always gets a slanted look of anger when one leaves during work hours, but I have the courage to ask repeatedly. Sermon about the rosary.

On Friday 5th October, I had to go to town to get a Typhoid vaccine. The last potatoes were dug up in the week. Yesterday, I didn't go to the fields until the afternoon. I took a pot of cabbage stew with me. Very cold and wet - I'm already wearing my knitted long pants.

On Thursday 4th October we heard of regulations about Germany. Again, I had hopes of seeing my beloved home in Gleiwitz again and of course, my loved ones. Even though my homeland may resemble a rubble desert, I will return home again. Obviously, we must get through the winter first.

My dear parents, you should see me like this. Sometimes, I look like a Russian vagrant. My hands are no longer recognisable, such as you have never had, Mutti.

Ach, I could write so much; how I think about everything, but I wouldn't know where to start. It is too much. I want to pour out all my thoughts to God. I haven't been to confession since Pentecost because what weighs on me, I can't tell of my soul in the five minutes before a service.

And apart from that, I haven't the right level of trust with each priest - not since Tepl.

Perhaps I'll write a little more today. If not, then we'll see each other next Sunday, my dear diary.

I'm thinking of you, my dears.

Your Youngest.

Wednesday 17th October 1945

Washed a lot of laundry today. It wasn't so bad because we had good wash powder.

Dear Mutti, now I know what you always did for us. You - for - us.

How good you were to us, dear parents.

Why has that realisation come so late?

Cried bitterly yesterday. Had trouble with Frau Beu.

Incredibly sad and had big homesick. And no Mutti here, to whom I could pour my heart out.

My God! Help me so I don't get lost in the stream of eight tormenting doubts, unanswered questions and gloomy thoughts. I have no-one with whom I can share, in words, all the things that are weighing on me. But I need someone spiritually related to me. I must find them soon. Then I would know an unheard, delicate togetherness; souls that understand each other without words. Not unlike how I warmed to Uncle Doctor May's family in the camp, because I recognised in them, something of myself. Oh, how I long for people, those with whom I was constantly together, like-minded people. There were good souls in our class. Where are you all, my beloved friends? Is there no-one looking for me?

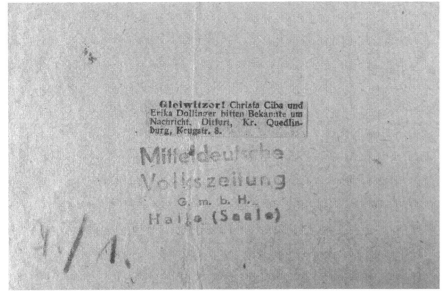

Advert asking for news from anyone from Gleiwitz who knows Christa-Maria and Erika, placed in regional newspaper, printed in Halle (Saale).

Sunday 21st October 1945, Lord's Day

Went to the service this morning. Spiritual sermon following the gospel of 22nd Sunday after Pentecost, about Christianity and politics. I am truly always happy when I listen to a good sermon.

When I think of the ones in Tissa, I don't know whether it is regarded as a sin, to consciously give such bad sermons.

Ach, I have so many questions that I cannot answer myself. Even though I have Erika, we're both still in the making and she doesn't have answers either. But I passionately believe I am not destined to be a maid forever, considering my life path so far, so I cannot and must not end up in a cow stall.

Lord, my God! Don't let me become that. Let me become what you have made me to become, for all eternity. If only that person could be found!

It seems to me that this is the current challenging time, a trial period, a time of probation, after which, having patiently survived, there will be different and better times again. Even though I have it good in so many ways - a bed to rest on, enough food to eat - I will never be truly satisfied with my situation here. That is why I'm firmly convinced that things will turn out differently, even if I look like a maid because of my weekday and Sunday clothes. It must be different.

I hope I can stay here over the winter. Of course, it's just embarrassing to set off in spring when one has let oneself be fed through the winter. With thanks, I'm thinking here of the farmers. I'm sure that's not entirely right either but what am I to do? Where am I to go when I have no-one and nothing......

Sunday 28th October 1945. Feast of Christ the King

Nice Sunday. Went to church in the morning. Went for autumn walk in the afternoon and then made music, with requests for dancing. Read in the evening, lovely food to eat. Torte for breakfast, jam and vanilla dip for dessert. What may have happened today in our Christ the King church service?

Started 'Macbeth' in the last week. I am happy to do some mentally stimulating work. One phrase is particularly unusual and interests me.

'There is still no art of reading the human soul in the face.'[34]

---

34 'There is no art to find the mind's construction in the face' Act 1, Scene 4. Macbeth, by William Shakespeare.

I thought about this and challenged myself on the field, whilst digging turnips and thought about a structure for it.

A) Main Part.
  1) What can you read in the face of your people?
  2) Where is man's soul revealed?
  3) Is man's soul to be found, completely?
B) Make no careless judgment.

Wednesday 31st October 1945

Helped in the kitchen with baking before lunch, for Frau Kramm's birthday tomorrow.

Worked cutting turnips in the afternoon. Yesterday, we only came back from the field at 20.30hrs.

Eight hundred turnips dug up today, the last of them.

Went to rosary devotions.

Tomorrow, 1st November. Who will lay flowers and light a candle on our family graves at home?

After how much silence in the cold earth, will there be recognition for those unknown and buried in a hurry? And you, my dears, who knows if you are in your forever silence already and no one stands at your grave on Holy Souls Day. No! No! That cannot be! I must find you again.

Dear God! Let us at least find each other once more.

CHAPTER TWENTY-ONE

Uncertainty for Ursula in Gera

1st November 1945

All Saints' Day. Church at 07.30hrs. In silent grief we remember our dearly departed, left in the homeland. Hilde surprises us with potato rolls.

2nd November 1945

All Souls' Day. Church at 08.00hrs. Vater goes with Hilde around Gera, looking for useful items in the ruins.

Onkel Josef sends news from Quedlinburg. I go to the town hospital.

3rd November 1945

Saturday work. Baked some rusks. Hilde in Leipzig. Vater in Schwaara. Bad mood.

4th November 1945

Lord's Day. Church at 07.30hrs. Rabbit and dumplings for lunch. Afternoon nap.

Frau Britta is invited for coffee with her little children.

5th November 1945

Today, I eagerly knit gloves for Hilde. Mutti goes back and forth to town.

6th November 1945

Nothing special. Hilde back from Leipzig.

7th November 1945

Parents in Rüsitz-Roben to get fruit. I went to town.

8th November 1945

Cold rainy day. Bad mood because I had to wear Vater's soaking wet coat.

9th November 1945

Vater went to Pölzig with Hilde. Harsh weather with a little snowfall.

Vater came back with booty that is nothing special.

10th November 1945

Saturday work. Fraulein Vogt from Eisenberg here.

11th November 1945

Lord's Day. Church at 07.30hrs. Early lunch, goose eaten, then afternoon nap. Hilde comes at 15.30hrs

12th - 13th November 1945

Nothing special.

14th November 1945

Today we sew a shopping bag at Frau Krähe's.

15th November 1945

Mutti has lots of washing to do. I go with Vater to get wood and coal. Terrible scrum.

16th November 1945

Vater went with Hilde to Pölzig. Pigs were slaughtered there. Mutti sewed again with Frau Krähe.

17th November 1945

Saturday work. Father in Rüsitz-Roben.

18th November 1945

Lord's Day. Church at 07.30hrs. Great dismay as we find our piece of roast pork was eaten by stray cats and dogs last night! Afternoon nap. Hilde here in the evening.

19th November 1945

In the morning, I was in town. Asked all the people we knew, who had come back from the west, but no-one could give precise information about Christel. Vater went to Eisenberg. I went to the Russian Commander in the afternoon, about our departure to West Germany.

20th November 1945

Today we receive post from Hannelore and Onkel Josef. I start, straightaway, to write a reply.

21st November 1945

Continue replying to the post - Tante Liesel, Hannelore, Curate Schenk, Uncle Josef and Liebenwerda Police Department; still no news of Christel.

22nd November 1945

Vater went early to see the Doctor. All went well there. Reply from Weimar!!!

23rd November 1945

Parents went to Pölzig in the morning. Got sugar beets.

24th November 1945

I went to the Wintergardens about our return to the English zone of West Germany.

Frau Beck asked us about her husband.

25th November 1945

Lord's Day. Church at 07.30hrs. Bishop from Ermland, (Warmia) expelled by the Polish, preaches today. Midday, Hilde is here, we have pork knuckle and dumplings for lunch. Afternoon nap. Parents then go to find people from Neustadt to see if they can get news of Oma Ciba.

26th November 1945

Holy Mass said for us. Otherwise, nothing special.

27th November 1945

Help Hilde with fetching wood, we get some for ourselves.

28th November 1945

Letter from Frau Herbert, where Tante Dorchen had been evacuated, reached us today. News of Christel's whereabouts! The joy over this news is great. Vater replied at once.

29th November 1945

Christel's nineteenth birthday. We go to church at 07.30hrs. Parents go to town.

30th November 1945

Morning in town. I buy knitting needles. Parents give post for Tante Dorchen to those returning from the West.

CHAPTER TWENTY-TWO

Christa-Maria in reflective mood

Sunday 4th November 1945. Ditfürt

Wrestled with myself until I asked for permission to go to prayer service today.

Every Sunday, it costs me my soul to ask, and I know the two others don't like to see me go and leave them to work. Extremely disappointed to find there was no Holy Mass because the clergyman from Quedlinburg was not there. The assembled prayed the joyous mystery of the rosary and then went home for their celebrations. Even though I couldn't go, I wanted to write it down, but I had to do Saturday-like cleaning of the fireplace before lunch. There was hammering and knocking in the yard all day long - and all this work on the Lord's Day!

Who suspects anything of what is going on inside me on Sundays? What must I do without? Who feels how hurt my heart was this morning?

In the afternoon, listened to Friedrich Schiller's birthday concert with fine musical accompaniment. I had to do darning whilst I listened so the farmers wouldn't see me, sitting there, doing nothing. How I long for something spiritual! To whom can I say that? Who understands where I'm coming from?

So, I was taken to complete joy when, last night, I dreamt of my dearest parents and Uschi!

If only such a dream could come true!

Wednesday 7th November 1945

Pig slaughtering - everything done and packed up in front of me. Wasn't disgusted or sick at sight of it. Mutti, you wouldn't recognise me. Ate like in Schlaraffenland.[35]

Thursday 8th November 1945

Took letter to Halle. Cleaned turnips. 7th - 9th November is a Russian holiday. Red flags decorate the Town Hall and are hung everywhere with pictures of Stalin. Everything communist. This is how my Fatherland now looks. Sad.

Saturday 10th November 1945

Cleaned turnips in the scullery. Washed my room in the evening.

Thought a lot about Friedbert.[36]

Sunday 11th November 1945. Lord's Day

Made juice. Didn't get to church this morning, so no Sunday today at the Kramm's. I must stop myself from saying something about that to them. In addition, it is questionable whether there will have been a service at all

---

35 Schlaraffenland refers to the Grimm Brothers' fairytale, 'The Land of Cockagne', a mythical land of plenty, excess and luxury, where everything is provided and requires no effort.
36 Friedbert is a friend from Gleiwitz mentioned earlier in Christa-Maria's diary on 13th July.

since the clergyman was not there last Sunday. It is said that he has already crossed the border to the West German side.

Thursday 15th November 1945

Loaded four baskets of food waste, peelings and bits cut from turnips that even the cows wouldn't eat. Received a dress, a jacket, a blouse, a nightie, two pairs of tights and an apron from clothes donated in the town. So, I won't freeze to death this winter either. Of course, they're old second-hand clothes that have been worn and nobody else wants - how would they come to me otherwise?

It is a year since I left my parents and my home. An entire year away from the homeland seems impossible to believe. What lies behind me with this year? Plenty of unbelievable hardships and it is true that I live as if in a dream. I don't know if the past was real or if this is my reality now. Are you who you were or who you are now? These troublesome questions, that have plagued me for a long time, are much in mind today.

Sunday 18th November 1945

Didn't go to church because I didn't know if there was a service or not, but at least I was able to enquire. I was cross with myself that I didn't leave as soon as I came down for breakfast, as it was still only 08.00hrs. I thought it was later. I think, today I just must blame myself for not going. So, I held my own Sunday service in my little room upstairs. Sunday must be a little different for me, not just like every other day of the week. I think about what I'll do the whole week. I must say that what I wrote in school, about concentration and distraction, for example, or about the attitude of the soul in general, I am only living it now. At home, I took great care not to reveal my innermost being, which is why I always resisted showing my essays to my parents, because in their eyes I wasn't as mature as my essays showed. On the other hand, I was able to reveal more of myself to Fräulein Erdhütter. However, not everything I wrote was untrue, as I had believed in the last few days that I was at home. What I wrote, has now become my truth and not just something for which I received a good grade.

I was very shocked, and annoyed at the same time, that, according to an essay in the Halle newspaper, Walter Flex[37] has heard that certain authors are being removed from library catalogues. Then, a sentence from Curate Schenk came to me: "Anyone who doesn't know Flex, knows not what kind of youth I long for."

Will the world suddenly no longer be our young world that Curate Schenk gave and entrusted to us? I can't find my way at all now and there is no one here who can answer my many long questions. Who understands me? When can I say, how it is in my inner turmoil, the peaks and troughs? Who knows anything about what is going on inside me, that I must deal with, all by myself? Lord God, help me forward. Let me find the Truth.

Tuesday 20th November 1945

Big laundry. In almost a year, had nothing there.[38]

I took my heart and told Mrs. Kramm. She helped me out of an extremely uncomfortable situation.

---

37 Walter Flex (1887 - 1917) was a German author and poet best known for his work 'The Wanderer Between Two Worlds,' a collection of poems reflecting his experiences as a soldier in WW2 and his search for meaning and purpose in a world shattered by war.
38 I believe this refers to having to wash bed linen because a period started unexpectedly after almost a year. Her periods would have stopped because she was malnourished and living under extreme stress for several months.

Mother, would you have put me in the wash tub on my days too? You spared us so much. I dream of you much more often now.

Thursday 29th November 1945

At Schneider's using their threshing machine.

Celebrated my birthday in the evening with four sorts of cake.

Thursday 29th November 1945, Ditfürt.

My beloved parents and Dear Uschi,

I cannot put into words how I am feeling on my 19th birthday.

To be honest, it's not like a birthday for me; I'm amazed at how I've held up so bravely for such a long time, before this day.

But when I saw how Frau Kramm tried to make this difficult day nice for me, I thought:

No! You cannot cry! Frau Kramm wants you to be happy, so let her succeed in making you happy. I was very pleasantly surprised that I could invite Erika (Dollinger) for coffee in the evening. There were four diverse kinds of cake! And that, in a time when famine stalks us like a ghost! I could hardly find words for this love shown to me on my birthday - a white bedecked table, Herr Kramm had his good shirt on; Frau Kramm, a real apron - and all to celebrate my day.

Obviously, I couldn't cry or be sad, so I chose to become happy instead.

Mutti dear, such cakes! With the best will in the world, you could not send me such cakes.

But I hope you don't misunderstand me; with gratitude and love, I remember my earlier birthdays, how my Mutti tried to please me. She did everything for me.

This birthday, I will carry with me for my whole life, wherever I am.

And so have you, my dear parents, created a lasting souvenir - I will always prove my worth to you and be worthy of your love.

Friday 30th November 1945

Spent the entire day in the barn.

Saturday 1st December 1945

Received a letter from Frau Herbert, in which stood Vater's address![39]

At first, I couldn't believe it!

I trembled whilst reading and quaked in my body and soul. I couldn't hold back the tears as it was hard to believe this joy, this happy message. Only now will I become myself again; too often I have asked myself, "Who are you. What are you?" I can hardly wait to see you again - whether it will be all four of us I don't know but I sing a song of thanks to the Lord.

The envelope and letter Christa-Maria received from her family.

---

39 An explanatory note about the letters: Tante Dorchen had been staying at Frau Herbert's house as a refugee. I don't know where this was. Christa-Maria had written to Tante Dorchen but by the time Christa-Maria's letter was delivered, Tante Dorchen had already moved on, leaving the Ciba Family address with Frau Herbert. In 1945, this was the network used to try and reconnect with family and friends; always leaving a forward address, if you had one, or at least the place you were hoping to reach and a general direction of travel.
Christa-Maria's letter to Tante Dorchen would have had her name and address as the sender, on the back of the envelope. Frau Herbert sent a letter to both the Ciba family in Gera and to Christa-Maria in Ditfürt, each having the other's address in it. They wrote to one another at once, their letters crossing in the post - their first communication with each other in over a year!

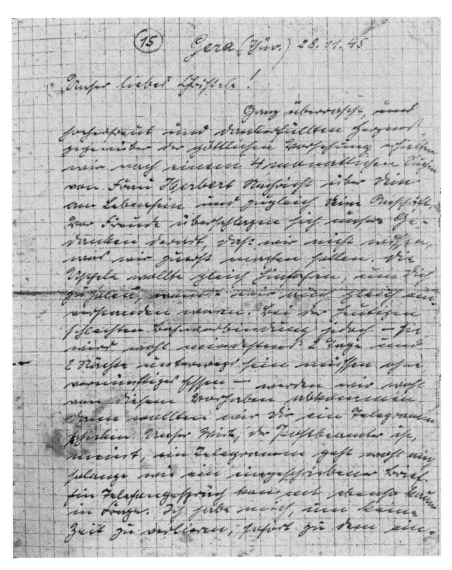

The first page of the letter Vater wrote, in Sütterlin, to Christa-Maria - their first contact in over 12 months.

Gera (Area 15) Thüringia. November 28ᵗʰ, 1945.

Our Dearest Christele,

Completely surprised, no, delighted and thankful for the divine rejuvenation, after four months of searching, we received news from Frau Herbert that you are alive! At the same time, in this letter, we see your address! It is with such joy our thoughts are racing; so much so, we don't know what to do first.

Uschela wanted to go there right away to get you. Though we also agreed at first, with today's bad train connections, however - she will probably have to be on the road for at least 2 days and 2 nights without reasonable food - we will probably not agree on this plan. Then we wanted to send you a telegram. Our contact will be the postal officer, who thinks a telegram probably takes as long as a registered letter. A telephone conversation is also hardly a possibility. I didn't lose any time to decide at once on the registered letter.

It will not reach you for your birthday itself but hopefully one day later 30.11. You will have this pleasure, dear child, certainly in consideration of the circumstances on the one hand, and the joy of our 'having found you' on the other hand. This letter will also later be the most beautiful birthday gift. At the same time, we wish you, as before, God's continued visible protection, health and everything else good for your new 20ᵗʰ year of life.

May you be spared all the disappointments experienced last year!

With our belief in God's divine care, we had a Holy Mass on 26ᵗʰ November - we can interpret this as a good sign for the new year of life as we wait now, starting to plan our seeing each other again. Well, we have experienced many things in 1945 up to our expulsion from Gleiwitz and thereafter - naturally, you can't begin to describe this properly, to give the true impression, in a letter. We keep these stories to tell when we see each other in person. We are now also looking forward to hearing of your experiences.

We don't intend to stay here either and wanted to continue to Bavaria. That can happen very quickly. Can you come to us soon? That would be the best. I get no notice here to move on. If you have no money, borrow 50 - 100RM from your host Familie Kramm and I will send the money to them at once. Oma Ciba stayed in Neustadt. She probably won't be well enough, unfortunately, to undertake such a journey over the winter.

We also don't know that she is still in Neustadt - Oma Ciba didn't respond to letters that we sent her when we were still Gleiwitz. In her last letter, Tante Dorchen had some harsh words for us, because we hadn't taken Oma Ciba with us. We clarified this in our reply to her; that we are innocent of causing this tragedy as it wasn't that we didn't want to take her with us. The good Lord knows this and, because we have asked for his understanding, will soon return Oma to us or to Tante Dorchen.

So, our dear child is coming soon! Mutti has baked Schrüpglützchen with Uschi, which represent your birthday and are waiting for you.

If there is a reason you can't come right away, then write it to us.

And we will send you the cookies in a package. About our stay, you will, yes, have already learned from Frau Herbert; because she writes to us that, along with her letter to us, she also sent one to you.

And now, in short, some addresses for you.

Josef Jurettko - Area 19. Quedlinburg, Neinbrücke 6, at Heiner's

Hans Herbst - Area 22 Kevelaer. Ventoerstrasse 89

Edi Reichel - Area 23 Ostercappeln l./Osnabrück, Kirchplatz 55, with Herr Kisling

Liesel Reichel - as above. Rosel Kahlert - as above

Luzie Trautmann - Area 21 Bielefeld. Friedhusser Strasse 32/2

Although unknown to us, send our greetings to the Kramm family and say thank you for the care they have shown you so far!

My dear sweet little one - on your 19th birthday I send you, from our new home, all my heartfelt birthday wishes and kisses. Bye! Until we see each other again. I have rescued some of your things and brought them here.

Your Uschi!

My dearest Christele,

In heartfelt thanks to our dear Lord, we have found each other!

Happy Birthday - have a big hug and kisses.

From your, Mutti

Sunday 2nd December 1945

No church service – church is closed. In the afternoon, finished off my humble advent wreath. Erika also made one. In the evening we had a fine advent celebration together. Read advent lesson from Curate Schenk:

Et erit in die illa lux magna, Alleluja.

And in that day, there will be a great light.

CHAPTER TWENTY-THREE

Letters of joy for Ursula!

1st December 1945. Gera

Saturday work. Fraulein Vogt from Eisenberg here. News of Christel from Frau Trautmann. I set about making an advent wreath.

2nd December 1945

Lord's Day. Church at 07.30hrs. Early lunch, then nap. Hilde comes with Pfefferkuchen to have with apple tea. She was also here for supper. Gloomy mood because of Vater's situation.

3rd December 1945

Nothing special.

4th December 1945

St. Barbara! Church at 07.30hrs with Mutti. Vater travels to Weimar - experienced all sorts there.

5th December 1945

Terrible weather. In the afternoon, I collect cherrywood branches.

6th December 1945

St Nikolaus! We baked some Pfefferkuchen for today. Vater went to Weimar again; today there is better news. Went to town with Mutti in the afternoon to cut the ski pants.

7th December 1945. Vater in Pölzig

Christel's first letter came today. Great was the joy!!!

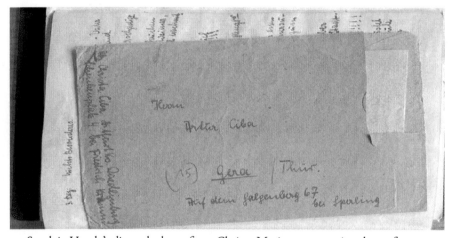

Stuck in Ursula's diary, the letter from Christa-Maria re-connecting them after 13 months of separation.

Ditfürt, 1ˢᵗ December 1945.

My Heart Loved Parents and Best Sisterlein,

Can it really be true that I have you again? I tremble so much with excitement and joy that I can barely write! The good Lord God has heard my innermost prayers for you. Praise and thanks be to Him. I can hardly believe this joy! I have always trusted and thought that, if He protected me so wonderfully, He would not abandon you.

I am well. I am with some dear and good farmers, I weigh 62kg. I have gorgeous food to eat and a lovely long, warm bed. I have been here since 29ᵗʰ August 1945. You have no need to worry over me. I hope you did not suffer too much from the many worries you've had for me. I always prayed, "Lord, be always close and give me your strength to endure the hardships." Hopefully, we can see one another again soon and lock our arms tightly around each other again. Be tenderly hugged and kissed from the depths of my joyful heart.

From,

Your Youngest.

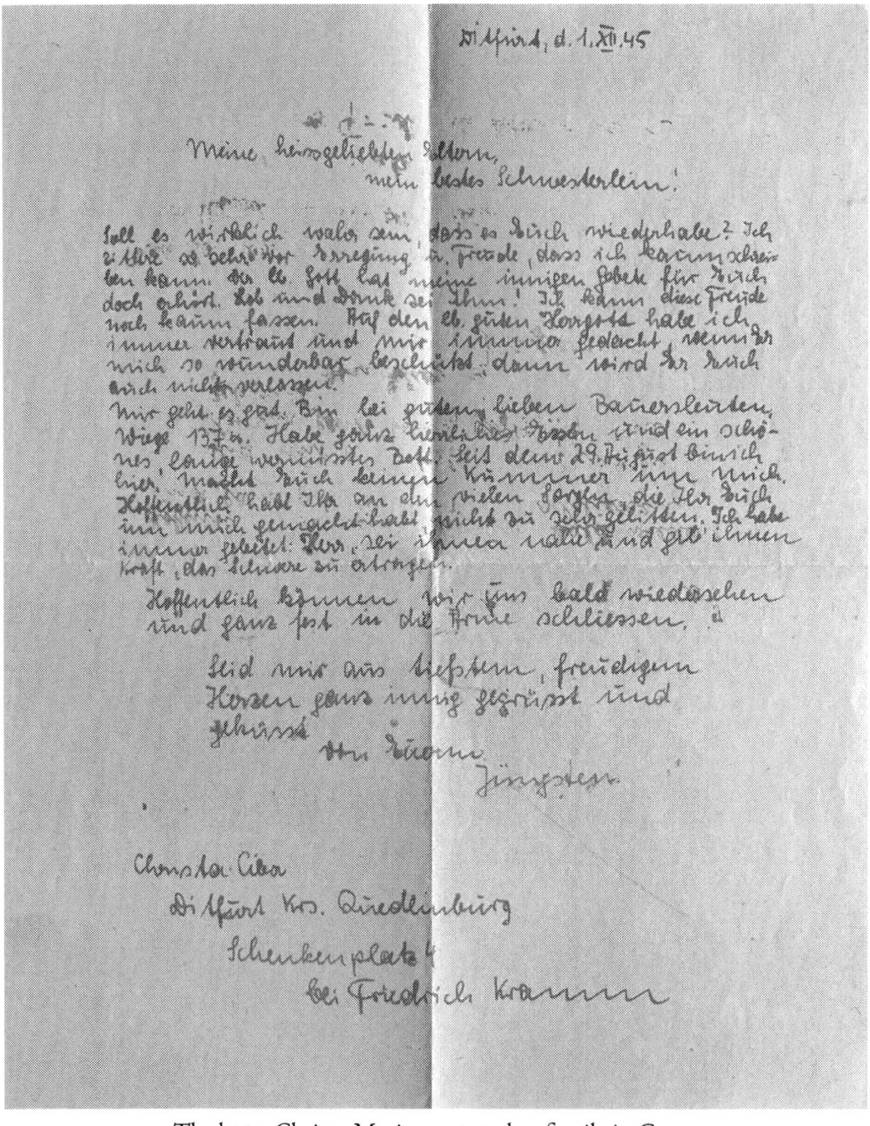

Ditfurt, d. 1.XII.45

Meine heissgeliebten Eltern,
mein bestes Schwesterlein!

Soll es wirklich wahr sein, dass ich Euch wiederhabe? Ich zittre so sehr vor Erregung u. Freude, dass ich kaum schreiben kann. Der lb. Gott hat meine innigen Gebete für Euch doch erhört. Lob und Dank sei Ihm! Ich kann diese Freude noch kaum fassen. Auf den lb. guten Herrgott habe ich immer vertraut und mir immer gedacht, wenn Er mich so wunderbar beschützt, dann wird Er Euch auch nicht verlassen.

Mir geht es gut. Bin bei guten, lieben Bauersleuten, Wage 137 [illegible]. Habe ganz herrliches Essen und ein schönes, lange vermisstes Bett. Seit dem 29. August bin ich hier. Macht Euch keinen Kummer um mich. Hoffentlich habt Ihr an den vielen Sorgen, die Ihr Euch um mich gemacht habt, nicht zu sehr gelitten. Ich habe immer gebetet: Herr, sei ihnen nahe und gib ihnen Kraft, das Schwere zu ertragen.

Hoffentlich können wir uns bald wiedersehen und ganz fest in die Arme schliessen.

Seid mir aus tiefstem, freudigem Herzen ganz innig gegrüsst und geküsst
von Eurer
Jüngsten.

Christa Ciba
Ditfurt Krs. Quedlinburg
Schenkenplatz 4
bei Friedrich Kramm

The letter Christa-Maria wrote to her family in Gera.

8th December 1945

Mary Immaculate Conception. Church at 08.45hrs. Afternoon coffee at Frau Britta's.

9th December 1945

Lord's Day. Church at 07.30hrs. We ate lunch early so the parents could go out looking for a room, as accommodation. In the afternoon, they went to Hilde for coffee. I stayed at home and wrote.

10th December 1945

Letter from Hannelore with news of Christel! Parents in town this afternoon.

11th December 1945

Christel came to us at about 13.00hrs!!!!!!

12th December 1945

Vater in Leipzig. Mutti is out with Christel to register in school, so she can catch up with her Abitur (A levels). I write a Christmas letter to Hannelore.

13th December 1945

Christel's first day at school, under 25's schoolchildren! A school where young German men in uniform were also trying to get the exam certificates they had been promised, when they enlisted.

Got some coal through Hilde - it came today.

14th December 1945

Vater in Pölzig with Hilde. Not much success.

15th December 1945

Saturday work - baking and cleaning.

16th December 1945

Lord's Day. Church 08.45hrs. (Confession.) Hilde there for lunch, parents go to Hilde for coffee. We both stay home, I write.

17th December 1945

Opa Ciba's birthday. He would have been 83yrs old! Early to Mass. I should go to see the doctor - big failure. Vater had to report to the employment office on the orders of the Soviet Military Administration - suddenly deciding we can cross the border to the West German side. Parents register us all to travel.

18th December 1945

Baked Pfefferkuchen. Mutti went again to Frau Krähe to sew. Apart from that, we had to do some laundry. I washed my hair. Transport goes on 20th December.

19th December 1945

There is a lot of running around with checking out and getting the car. I must get one from Debschwitz. Vater goes to Roben to get apples and a rabbit. Package for Onkel Josef is going by express this morning.

20th December 1945

Church at 07.30hrs. Our travel day! Parents still have things to do in town this morning. With Christel, I quickly pack everything together. Frau Britta comes to say goodbye. Journey begins 16.30 - 16.50hrs. The journey is long; we travel the whole night through until 12.30hrs the next day, always in the van. In Arenhausen, where the border crossing is to take place..........

21st December 1945

The border is already closed when we arrive; therefore, we must go to the refugee camp - a freezing pigsty. Corrugated iron barracks. At night, we freeze miserably. I sit next to a small oven nearly the whole time. Vater's last hat was stolen in the camp.

22nd December 1945

After the English Generals had been to Heiligenstadt for a meeting, during which time we were kept behind barbed wire and guarded by the Russians, we made our way to the border barrier at 10.30 - 11.00hrs. The border crossing itself is peaceful, we are not checked ourselves, but the 10km walk to the camp on the English side is difficult. After a short search by guards at the Friedland camp and getting rations for the march, we are still booked on the special train, in which every window is missing, going to Ahlen/Westphalia at 17.00hrs today.

23rd December 1945

Lord's Day. We will be unloaded in Ahlen at around 05.30 - 06.00hrs. The parents get the camp rations while we stay with our luggage. With empty freight train going back to Friedland, we were taken as far as Bielefeld. In the Christian hostel we are given a room for one night. After a refreshing sleep we visit Frau Trautmann.

24th December 1945

The parents have some things to take care of - getting food ration stamps and finding somewhere to stay. We can stay at the hostel for a few more nights. I go with Vater to get some of our things from the station; we meet Werner Bartsch who used to join us at our cabin by the swimming pool in Richtersdorf near Gleiwitz.

Christmas Eve! Unlike any other! Bread and butter in the hostel before midnight mass. Christel unable to sing 'Stille Nacht' with tears rolling down her cheeks in church.

25th December 1945

Christmas Day! Church at 08.00hrs. We went for lunch at the 'Bristol' (10RM)

In the afternoon we are invited to the Trautmann's apartment for coffee and supper.

26th December 1945

Boxing Day! Church at 10.00hrs. We eat in the cellar at the town hall for lunch.

Afternoon nap, then I write.

27th December 1945

Nothing special. Vater goes to the office. Herr Trautmann visits us in the morning. We must go with Mutti to the station to fetch a blanket from our bigger pieces of luggage that are still there. Parents go to the Trautmann's in the evening.

28th December 1945

Vater travels early to Münster, to the state tax office.

29th - 31st December 1945

Nothing special happened. New Year's Eve celebrated in silence and solitude.

Ursula's diary entry for the day Christa-Maria arrived is so brief. I expect you may be asking the question, 'Is that it?'

You must make what you will of all the exclamation marks following that simple statement,

'Christel came to us today at about 13.00 hrs!!!!!!

The relief, joy and cumulative exhaustion of the previous twelve months was beyond words, when they were finally reunited. As my mother had written in her diary during 1945,

'When one feels much, one says little.'

The burden of their experiences was wrapped up and weighed so deeply within, neither sister had the desire or need to continue writing a daily diary, now they were together again and getting on with their lives. The simple things we often take for granted became their daily fight for survival in Gera - queuing for food, keeping warm, finding somewhere to sleep with a roof over their heads - whilst waiting for their opportunity to cross from East to West Germany en route to Bielefeld in the British controlled zone of northwest postwar Germany.

From conversations I had with my mother, I know she left the Kramm's farm in Ditfürt to travel the 120km to Gera by train, a long, fractured journey taking several days. She told me how, with the help of a street map picked up from a station kiosk, she walked across town to 67, Galgenberg Strasse and simply knocked on the door of the Sperling family, who had taken them in, hoping to find someone there. On seeing her parents and sister again, she noticed how thin they were, having starved under Russian, then Polish rule and while fleeing their home. They were so delighted and grateful to be together again in Bielefeld, after a year of separation.

I like to imagine them sitting at a perfectly laid table, sharing their experiences after a meal together, as they might have done before the war.

In truth, this didn't happen - perhaps none of them wanted to relive any of the trauma of the previous twelve months. In December 1945, the Ciba family still lived like refugees and despite reaching safety in Bielefeld on 23rd December 1945, the years to come were harsh and dreary, living in cramped accommodation with what precious little food there was, being rationed and hard to come by.

Ursula continued her diary from 1946 - 1950, as an annual summary, which I have included here to complete the translation of her diary.

CHAPTER TWENTY FOUR

Aftermath 1946 - 1950

1946

It has been three months since I last wrote in my diary, and I must say they have been long difficult months. We had to cope with all the adversities in our "new home" that followed the war, which had ended unhappily for us. They rattled us repeatedly, to continue their gruelling work but we had to finish it.

So, on my 21st birthday, 12th April 1946, I, Ursula, renew my promise and catch up on recording the last 3 months.

It seems almost impossible, despite all efforts and tireless work of the parents, to get a suitably furnished room with cooking facilities. Then it was Vater's birthday - how sad it was on this day, when I think back to the lovely celebrations we had in previous years - Gleiwitz! But I won't shy away from at least pleasing Vater with a cake, which I of course brought, unnoticed, to our room in the hostel. A daring undertaking without any kitchen appliances. Well, it had been possible to roll the dough out with a beer bottle and it went rather well! We were able to finish it off at the baker's oven and the coffee, secretly brewed on an electric cooker, added to the celebrations.

Middle of January, I was invited to go with Erna Grosse-Boymann to her old home in Essen-Bredeney. I was delighted with her parents' apartment, which was already in good order and peaceful again. Frau G-B managed to make the day pleasant and varied in every respect. However, I was saddened by Mausi's behaviour, that had developed since her flight from Gleiwitz and which, despite our ten-year friendship in Upper Silesia, she showed on many occasions while I was there. Unfortunately, the fateful year of 1945 has passed over her without shaping her into the kind of human being that the needs of our time demand: To have complete dedication and ultimate commitment to the future. Pity that it has come to this...

By the time I got home, the parents had found a furnished room with an understanding landlord. A lady from the hostel, Mina Kahre, has a small apartment at 59, Ehlentrupper Weg. She says we can stay there. At Mina Kahre's apartment, we share one room. It has a double bed, two small sofas, a table and chairs, where Christa will have to study, and a one-ring hot plate so we can at least boil some water!

The following weeks were tough because it was winter again. Frozen fingers still show traces of not being able to warm up for days. It wasn't easy to hold it together in these weeks; in addition to the extreme cold was the excessive shortages of bread and food stuffs.

At the end of February, Vater goes to Tante Dorchen and Onkel Hans in Kevelaer. Here, he lives in the 'land of milk and honey' and quickly recovers well. His stay was too short only because his reinstatement took place on 8th March 1946. Tante Dorchen and Onkel Hans also looked after Vater's 'three women' in a touching way; they knew what basic things we were missing and supported us. Even today, they are helpful to us in every way they can be, otherwise we would go hungry on some days. During Vater's absence, I started to make a sweater, skirt and jacket with the wool that we brought from home. I am working with love and enthusiasm, happy to see the constant progress of my efforts. My main occupation here, as in Gera, is the honourable task of taking care of the household, while Mutti goes out, constantly, to find vegetables and to redeem our food vouchers.

Christel eagerly attends her Abitur (A level) courses. She has settled in well but learning without the proper books and in our single, small, shared room is not easy. For me, it was the time to make a career choice or, I should say, time to look for a position. In addition to the applications for admission to the Paderborn teacher training college, there are also applications for admission to the hospitals and factories.

So far, I haven't heard anything positive from any of them. I must wait, patiently; the question of employment is often a great worry for me - I don't really know what I should begin. It is pretty much the same for the classmates I have found again. We all want to find work.

We are deeply saddened to learn from Tante Elly, on Onkel Josef's birthday, that he was admitted to hospital in Quedlinburg with a nervous breakdown on 26th February 1946. All the following news about the health of our good Onkel Josef is encouraging though - he has been suffering with a high fever for weeks and has had ten litres of water taken from him. Daily, our thoughts are with you, dear Onkel Josef. We say the rosary for your rapid return to good health and strength to you, dear Tante Elly and dear 'Da-Da' (*Jochen.*) Your last news, that Onkel Josef had been fever-free for two days, seemed happy and peaceful, dear Tante Elly. We dare to hope that you are recovering, dear Onkel Josef. The next letter from Tante Elly brought good news, thank God.

Suddenly, there was also a decisive turn for me about finding a job: On 6th June 1946, I started work in Bielefeld at Dr. August Wolff's firm, a big chemical business. At first, I worked in the laboratory on the unit calculation of trypsin - a protein-splitting fermentation process. Some of the work involved calculations I hadn't learnt at school due to lack of time. For example, to prepare and adjust the concentration of a solution.

At Pentecost in this year, we're visited by Onkel Josef and Tante Dorchen, who had really helped us, which was a pleasant way to spend the holidays. It was wonderful on those days, even though the whole festive hustle and bustle took place in our 'ostentatious' one-roomed apartment. Christel and I go to Piepenstock Detunder Street to sleep - they are kind enough to take us as overnight guests during the Pentecost holiday.

The celebrations passed quickly and were exchanged, once again, with me in my new working environment.

As the summer months passed over the country, I spent my free time rejoicing in the Teuteburger forest, foraging for fruits, herbs and mushrooms.

Again, I receive news about the lives of fellow classmates. Great is the joy, each time, when we hear that, slowly, slowly they are reunited with their parents......... and at the beginning of August, I hear from Hannelore, that Wolfhart is reportedly in a Czech prisoner of war camp. I am so happy to hear news of him, although not the best circumstances, because we hadn't heard from each other since December 1944. One day, the expected letter from Wolfhart himself, fluttered into our 'house'. My greetings, which I sent at once on the reply card, should be a small joy for Wolfhart in his monotonous and surely exhausting prisoner life. Hopefully, our common wish, that he returns safe and well to Germany, will come true for him.

19th September 1946

Today is a very meaningful day for Christel - she takes her oral English Abitur (A level) and is beaming with joy at the success she has achieved. Back home, now that it's done, unfortunately no popping champagne corks to celebrate such an occasion, as was the case for me in April 1943. The Russians have also made us poorer in terms of our wine and champagne supplies....... and we have yet to regain our wealth.

We hear from Quedlinburg that Onkel Josef left hospital, in July 1946, in good health and can return to work part-time. As much as we are delighted by this news, the joy is marred by the fact that Tante Elly has herself been admitted to hospital. How we would like to be with you in these difficult days and to help you.

Furthermore, we receive a telegram from Kevelaer on 6th July. It says that up to now, Oma Ciba stays in Holthausen/Oldenburg. Tante Dorchen and Mutti travel in the next few days to fetch Oma and bring her to Bielefeld. We celebrate this reunion! Then Oma moves to Kevelaer with Tante Dorchen and Christel goes there for a few days.

I have changed my first job at the Wolff laboratory and now work with mice in the insulin analysis laboratory. During my first few days there, I was with the white mice all the time - I practically lived there. I found this work extremely interesting, learning how to carry out unit calculations and adjust the insulin solution after conscientious testing with the mice.

Right in the middle of the daily routine of our miserable lives, getting food and keeping warm, we received the painful news of Onkel Josef's sudden death on 2nd October 1946. We could not grasp then, in our heartache and grief, news from Jochen of his mother's (*Tante Elly*) death on 7th October 1946. The words of the eulogy for our dearly deceased, who continue to live on in our memory, having passed away from this earthly vale of tears, will comfort us in our deep sadness.

'In Christ, the hope of blessed resurrection shines. The inevitable and unchangeable fate of death weighs heavily on us, but the promise of eternal life, lifts us up. Lord, the life of your faithful servants cannot be taken away; it is merely transformed. Now, their earthly life has crumbled to dust and a new home awaits them in Heaven.'

Mutti takes on all the hardship and plans to go to Quedlinburg in mid-October, dressed in her black clothes of grief. There, she must speak further with Jochen. He should come to Bielefeld, where we can take care of him. Mutti comes back alone this time because Jochen has some errands to attend to in Quedlinburg. He manages to cross the border from east to west Germany, also in his grief-black, and reaches us in early November. It must be hard for him, to find himself suddenly an orphan; his beloved and ever-caring parents taken from him, at such an early age. But I think this sad fate has not registered with him yet; perhaps it is good that it is so, that he doesn't carry his loss so hard.

Jochen Jurettko as a baker's apprentice in Bielefeld.

Jochen doesn't continue at school here in Bielefeld.

He will become a baker. After many hopeless efforts, Vater manages to find him a place as a baker's apprentice where he will start 2nd January 1947.

For Christel's 20th birthday, we have an enjoyable time together with Frau Trautmann.

It becomes winter and the Teuteburger forest now stands in white splendour and all the houses have put on snow caps. Everywhere, the children enjoy the many, white feather-flakes that Mother Nature shakes down. It all looked so charming and homely......ah, home; but it is only a dream, that we dream repeatedly, of the home we left and now long for.

In December 1946, I travelled to Kevelaer for a few days. On the way back, I take a boat along the Rhine from where I can see closely the impressive gothic structure of Cologne Cathedral. Unfortunately, I don't have time to admire the interior, where builders work to repair the enormous bomb damage. My few days in Kevelaer were genuinely nice. Again, they passed by all too quickly as is always the case with joy-filled holidays.

24 - 25 - 26th December 1946
Holy Christmas Feast days.

Again, this year the 'Gloria in Excelsis Deo' of the angelic host announces to us, just as it did to the fearful shepherds in Bethlehem, the birth of the Lord. Let us all, earnestly, ask the divine child for His infinite love and true Christmas joy for all people.

We come to this year's Christmas feast days far happier and with many of last year's worries lifted from us, when we had left Gleiwitz and were longing for our house and home. Still, the longing comes at times like this.

I go with Christel to a Christmas Mass in the Liebfrauen Church, which is to be celebrated by a visiting English priest, in English, for the English people here. However, this Midnight Mass did not really connect me with the holy events of this night; not like the beautiful Christmas Mass in the Queen of Peace chapel in previous years, where Curate Schenk led the service. Hopefully, we can be together again, one day, for this Christmas celebration.

We spent New Year's Eve quietly and wished for joy in the coming New Year.

Letter from Mutti, Margarete Ciba (Gretel) in Bielefeld to Rosel Kahlert and the Reichel family in Ostercappeln.

Bielefeld, 18th August 1946.

My Dears,

First, to you, dear Rosel, thank you so much for providing us with 'pudding powder'. Hopefully, this will help with the procurement of food here. We very much welcomed the increased allocation of food because the last rations of bread and potatoes were completely incorrect. It is also unbelievably bad with the vegetable allocation. We only get 0.5 kg per person per week. Hopefully, the time will soon come again, when we can buy these basic foods in free trading for everyone. The trees in the gardens are richly blessed with fruit. Owners only want to 'sell' in exchange for something else and since we have nothing, we often go empty-handed.

Still, we found some fallen apples.

It is becoming increasingly difficult to find housing for refugees here because the influx has not ended yet. The Bavarians are expelling

Silesian refugees. We heard about the Bavarian approach from several sides. We have been alone in the apartment for eight days. Fraulein Kahre has been away for a few days. At times, it felt as though we were in our own place and could switch things round, make changes we wanted; unfortunately, it will be a long time before we are able to be in our own home.

How is Bärbel Kahlert doing? Has the Tuberculosis been cured and is she completely well again?

Is the holiday season ending for Franz and Reinhard? Christel was only on holiday for two weeks! Her written work for her Abitur (A levels) begins tomorrow. The lack of books and our cramped living conditions make preparing for these exams exceedingly difficult. In the Russian Zone, the high schools ceased to exist after the holidays and were replaced with primary schools. Everything in Germany is being redesigned according to the different principles of the English, American, French and Russian zones.

How are you dear Liesel and dear Edi? Hopefully, you are healthy after all you have been through.

We wish Frau Kahlert (*Josef Kahlert's mother, Ottilie*) a good recovery from tuberculosis, while she stays with you. Rosel will do her utmost and do everything possible to improve Frau Kahlert's health.

So, I will close now and leave heart-felt greetings for all your loved ones.

Your Gretel.

In the same envelope, a few lines from Vater, Artur Ciba.

This note, handwritten in Sütterlin script, had a piece missing, ending the letter abruptly, either torn away or nibbled by mice. It was sent to me in 2020 by Franz Kahlert, along with the letter above, written to his mother, Rosel, by Margarete Ciba, my Oma. Interestingly, the original letter is dated 1945 which I know to be wrong - My mother pointed out it must have been written in 1946 - I have changed the date on the translated version here.

All my loved ones!

A few lines from me too. First, I want to inform you that I received my denazification[40] a few days ago and can therefore continue to work. In addition to my writing and our testimonies, Edi's (Eduard Reichel) testimony has certainly contributed to this successful outcome. Thank you, again, dear Edi, for that. Divine providence has intervened for me and for all of us, as has been so often the case since January 1945. We have been blessed with this help for almost one-and three-quarter years. God's goodness must be praised repeatedly, at every opportunity. I will tell you more about the denazification process later.

In any case, one worry has been lifted from us. The mountain of worries which were piled high when we escaped from Gleiwitz a year ago, gradually gets smaller. Now our main concerns are namely the supply of

---

40 Denazification was an Allied Forces initiative to rid German and Austrian public office of Nazi ideology, following the end of the Second World War. After the Potsdam Agreement in August 1945, each Allied zone took responsibility for the process. It was carried out by removing those who had been Nazi or SS officials from positions of power and influence, disbanding organisations associated with Nazism and trying prominent Nazis for war crimes in the Nuremberg Trials in 1946. What began as a diligent and essential process for the future of Germany soon became delayed and deprioritised due to the sheer number of cases and lack of officials to process them. The process was more lenient in West Germany than in Soviet controlled East Germany, the French zone being the most lenient. Germans had to answer a questionnaire (Fragenbogen) to assess their activities and level of involvement during Nazi rule. Five categories were set up - Major Offenders, Offenders, Lesser Offender, Followers and Exonerated Persons. As the Fragenbogen was completed in German and processed by Allied personnel without sufficient language skills, it was decided to involve Germans. In March 1946, the 'Law for Liberation from National Socialism and Militarisation' came into effect, turning over the denazification process to the Germans. The Americans continued their efforts to denazify Germany through control of German media - the Information Control Division took control of newspapers, radio stations, theatres, cinemas, book publishers, printers and libraries. For many, including my grandfather, Artur Ciba, the process now needed a different questionnaire, statements and testimonies from others about levels of involvement. These statements were nicknamed 'Persilscheine' and refer to adverts for the whitening laundry detergent, Persil. Until in possession of a denazification certificate, Artur Ciba was unable to work in any official role and could only do manual labouring tasks to earn any money. In 1951, the provisional West German government granted amnesties to lesser offenders and ended the programme.

food and rebuilding a humble home of our own. The main task is to survive these times and keep in good health, which, thank God, seems to be the case for us.

About the mixed money that Frau Kahlert returned: I will report to my mother in the next letter I send to her.

Have you been able to gather and store some fruit? We already have five mason jars: not much, but at least it's something.

Had we been in Gleiwitz for the start of Christel's Abitur (A levels) tomorrow, as in the old days, we would have treated her with cookies, chocolates and a dash of a tonic drink to boost her energy ready for her exams.

1947

The coming year, with its most notable events, should again be in the form of diary entries, 'to be remembered' ...... can I partially recall this year and finish with a happy conclusion?!?!?

On my birthday, I would again like to close the gap since the last notes and briefly report on what I have experienced so far. Until the beginning of March, a cold, sharp winter with quite a lot of snow, ice and the grim cold, well known to us from our old homeland, is a constant companion.

In contrast to last year, we are doing a little better despite the large, long-lasting freezing weather, because last summer we were able to build up a modest supply of wood and coal. Christel has been working for the director, Mr. George Trimming, at the Reichs Bahn (railways) in the interpreter's office since the beginning of the year, and I have a pleasant warmth in our offices at the laboratory, which is quite an enviable advantage now, in the freezing weather.

Father, on the other hand, isn't so pleasantly warm in any office, and yes, Mutti freezes again in the one-room apartment until late in the afternoon, when we can manage to light a fire despite all the obstacles. Oh, coal rich Heimat, why are you so far away???

For Oma Ciba's 75th birthday, Vater and Mutti went to Kevelaer to celebrate this day of honour together with Vater's birthday, in a small group, with Tante Dorchen and Onkel Hans.

Uschi Przemeck's marriage on 18th February 1947 in Padingbrüttel-Wesermünde to Josef Rüst from Gleiwitz is one of the notable events of the new year. She is the first from our Gleiwitzer group to suddenly have a completely new, distinct set of duties. May the Lord bless her husband, grant her true family happiness and peace.

In the middle of March, I take some of my holidays from the previous year and take a six-day break in Frankfurt am Main. I am happy to travel there to see Marga and Ursula Rüst, whom I haven't seen for two years. After a reasonable journey in a crowded train, I arrived in Frankfurt at about 19.00hrs and soon, I was with Marga again! It was a blissful moment when we stood face to face and could embrace each other, beaming with joy, in the old friendly way. Of course, there was no end to the storytelling because we both had an overwhelming amount to report on from our individual experiences of the last two years. The blissful, wonderful school years that we keep mentioning, in our beloved homeland with our various memories, keep us chatting together, each beautifully delivering our stories. The following Sunday, Marga and I surprise the new Frau Ursula Rüst at her humble home in Mühlheim am Main. I had yet to give my thoughtful wedding gift - a small rubber plant - to her. Here again, our reunion was wonderful, so full of homely familiarity. Uschi's husband set up a mail order business for office equipment and stationery there, despite many difficulties, and tries to ensure a happy family life for Uschi. I spent some more time with Uschi in Frankfurt and Offenbach where we visited Hannelore.

During this holiday season I was able to get to know a region of our fatherland that was known to me only from my Vater's stories and Goethe's descriptions in 'Poetry and Truth'.

It was just sad that the city of German handicrafts lost so much of its ancient, vibrant buildings to the bomb terror. My departure day approached too quickly. Happy with all I'd managed to achieve, on a budget, I travelled back to Bielefeld. March 29th is my first day of work, and time is going briskly again in the insulin evaluation laboratory, towards the Easter holidays. We were able to celebrate the holidays in good health and with all sorts of festive preparations. Unfortunately, shortly after Easter, the head of our insulin evaluation department, Fräulein Dr. Schober was moved to a new job. I worked well with her, and she understood me while we were together, maybe because she is also a refugee from the East. This change is the result of the constant disagreements of the company's insulin chemists. I still don't get along very well with the new work manager, and I don't believe that we will ever have such a pleasant relationship between superiors and subordinates, despite all our efforts.

Luckily, my birthday this year was work-free. I was particularly pleased with Wolfhart's snowdrops greeting card from the southeast which I received on this day. The following time is filled with the joyful expectation of the approaching spring with its urgent and revitalising rays of sunshine. The next few weeks pass quickly without anything worth mentioning, until two weeks before Pentecost, Tante Dorchen and Onkel Hans visit us here for three days. Shortly thereafter Miss Dr. Britta, now in Elze-Hauss, comes to see us. Dear visitors from Gleiwitz, we are always particularly pleased to see you, despite all the inconveniences that our 'expelled life' brings with it. We are alone for this year's Pentecost festival, Jochen is with us for some of his free time.

I would like to report on an event that happened during my work in the laboratory, which is not quite ordinary. Glistening fullness of light surrounds us....... There is to be filming in the laboratory and the picture reporters start with their big shots for the world in film. We've all been eagerly awaiting the launch for weeks. After four weeks, the big 'premier' will take place, which we will experience together. Although I was already used to being filmed at home, the preparations, the recordings themselves and then the possibility of failure when the film strip was running through the projector, brought me some fast heartbeats.

In the following weeks, it really seems to be true that we are to get our own apartment!!

It is not difficult for someone who finds themself in the same situation, to understand what hurdles must be overcome and what exertions are associated with a move, especially in these challenging times. Vater has been hard at work for months to give the 'four walls' of our future apartment a homely, cosy look. Although a fall into the depths, from our former home in Gleiwitz to the present one, we must be thankful for everything that we already own again, as property. After the most necessary preparatory work, the move could start without the need for an 8m long furniture van. So, we get our new home in the first weeks of August. Now we live in two rooms, a kitchen and a glass veranda on the ground floor at 31, Frobel Strasse, Bielefeld. We must give up a third room belonging to this apartment and the bathroom is now offered as a kitchen. We are all happy we are no longer sub-tenants in a small space and Mutti is of course delighted to be able to work in her own kitchen. After a short time in our new home, Oma Ciba pays a surprise visit. She will probably stay here for the summer!

I've been looking forward to my vacation for a long time, which I'm happy to be able to spend on the Baltic Sea again. How longingly I had wished to have such a holiday in our last years at home, especially since we last had such joys in 1939. Now, with the work of moving to our new home, I couldn't think of anything nicer to do! So, on 21st August 1947, I go on my holidays, grateful that I can travel freely after everything we lived through in 1945. On 29th August, I have the special joy of being able to make a short trip to Switzerland. I had a wonderful time and enjoyed telling my parents, Christel and Oma all about it. I was happy with a new lust for life as I went back to work in the laboratory, working with rabbits because white mice are no longer available to us. Work puts on a big Autumn festival and not long after that, in the first week of November, our laboratory hosts a party for company friends, which was magnificent! Yes, it is good to experience such evenings after a year of demanding work.

It is still mild at the end of November, and we are not freezing like last year with frost and icicles. Some snow fell but melted in a few hours, then it rained the entire day, then the sun shone from 8am - 12pm the next day. The warm sun on our ground floor flat and the mild weather in December is quite pleasant; otherwise, it would have been unbearable in our apartment. In the cold and wet weather, the kitchen, which we don't even heat because of the bad stove, is extremely uncomfortable, cold and damp. Christel suddenly moves to Frankfurt am Main with her work as interpreter for the reconstruction of the railways, now to be known as Deutsche Bundesbahn (DB) on 15th December 1947 - so soon before Christmas - but she is excited about it. Yes, she also wants to live a little again. We spend Christmas with Jochen. Christel only comes back from Frankfurt for the first time, on Christmas Eve. Jochen and I cut a small Christmas tree from the Teuteburger forest, and I also looked out for some smaller branches and pinecones to make a festive table decoration.

Healthy and satisfied with life, we spent Christmas Eve together and brought joy to one another with the exchange of small practical gifts. We all attended this year's English Christmas Mass and were impressed by the festive tone this year. On the first day of the holidays, Frau Ziegert and Inge came to see us. We sing Christmas carols together and tell stories of good times from our home in Gleiwitz. On the second day of the holidays, we are invited to the Blüme family for afternoon 'Kaffee und Kuchen'. New Year's Eve we spend peacefully at home.

1948

For the third time after the cruelly forced departure from my homeland, on my birthday this year, I am adding the events of the new year to what has already been written here in this diary.

We feel wonderfully comfortable in our new home and the mild winter contributes, in part, to that. With one or two newly added pieces of furniture, a very cosy arrangement is possible! Christel is often in Bielefeld again, so that she doesn't notice much that she's left. Apart from that, there is variety at home for the parents with the frequent visits from dear friends from Gleiwitz. Some days the coming and going doesn't stop, there's always an awful lot of news to catch up on.

No significant changes have occurred in the laboratory; after the working hours, a cosy get-together brings balance to the variety of minds that often clash at work. So, a really nice carnival evening - which I didn't want to go to at first - but then I let myself be persuaded by many words - brought us much closer together again; and I had a good time dressed in a geisha costume, in spite of the fact the host didn't participate from the first time we were together!!!

The celebrations did not seem to end before Easter: On March 5 1948, I was invited as bridesmaid to a colleague's wedding here in Bielefeld. Obtaining a wedding gift and a long dress for me is a lot of trouble and a headache. Yes, I never thought that I would attend my first wedding as an adult in Bielefeld.

Any further invitation to a similar celebration will obviously no longer pose any difficulties for me about what to wear! Exactly one week later, the next marriage, of a laboratory colleague, took place. There might have been something going on at Uschi Niehoff's pre-wedding party; a celebration like this, in the house, would not have been allowed otherwise. It would have been of the demurer type that is characteristic for a young bride. I ended up at home well after midnight, even a little drunk; getting up and staying in the lab the next day was difficult for me, especially since there was a lot of work to do.

We were able to spend the Easter holidays healthy, all together and enjoyed walks through nature, freed from the ice. The warm spring sunshine entices the buds to bloom, making delicate, decorative displays of blossom for the holidays. A week after Easter, a wonderful time begins for me: I'm taking my summer vacation from last year and visiting Christel in Frankfurt. Christel herself was very tense and had little time for shared experiences, but I had plenty to do and could spend precious time with Marga, Uschi Rüst and Hannelore. So, I was able to be with Marga, Uschi Rüst and Hanne Jany again. I attend several lectures at the university and was involved in sports at the university institute. There, I met the colleagues of Professor Hückel - from the experimental chemistry department in Breslau, Miss Dr. Wense and Rosmarie Hübrich from Gleiwitz. Last year I had already spent time in the city, so we were quite familiar with the old town with its red sandstone buildings, which are worth seeing and well-known from Goethe's 'Poetry and Truth'. The

Paulskirche will be worked on day and night to be completed for the centenary celebrations. A meeting with Fräulein Erdhütter, who works in the high school in Bingen, took place in Rüdesheim during my vacation time. We were able to spend a beautiful sun-drenched Saturday (10th April) together.

The much praised and often visited vineyards of this small Rhine town did not interest us so much, since there was nothing of the delicious drink available. We enjoyed, much more, the surroundings. A hike through the still bare vineyards led us to the Niederwald monument, which still enjoys its original location in full size and thus points to France. Built 1870 - 1871, to commemorate the founding of the German Empire after the Franco-Prussian war, it is a massive statue of Germania, the symbol of German unity. Overlooking the Rhein and Mosel valleys, the views were stunning. On the Sunday before my birthday, I travelled to a high-altitude health resort with Christel in Königstein am Taunus. We prayed at Bishop Kaller's grave and then attended the high mass in the parish church. There we heard a rousing sermon by a Jesuit priest (Johannes Brassek JS, last heard in Lübeck) on the subject of 'worship and worship of God'. We had lunch in the Königstein spa restaurant and sat in the sun in the spa gardens. In the afternoon, we organised an evening climb in the old ruins of Königstein Castle. An experience there! Christel handed me a gift on the high castle tower, which almost blew away in a wild gust of wind!! Still impressed by this strange happening yesterday, we took leave of Königstein. For my birthday, we went to church in the morning - I had to thank God the Father for many beautiful and good things and to beg him again for the fulfilment and answering of many requests - Christel prepared me a good birthday coffee and had made me a birthday table with very small traveling treasures - one pair of nylon stockings, soap and face cream. Only Wolfhart's bouquet of flowers was missing; actually it was there. The order travelled from Yugoslavia, first to the East, then to Bielefeld and finally to Frankfurt where, unfortunately, I didn't receive a nice bouquet. In the afternoon we celebrated my birthday in a relaxed way with Uschi Rüst and Marga, even with cake and potato salad for the evening. Mutti had given all these goodies to Mr. Rücker, who was in Bielefeld last weekend.

The last few days of vacation went by quickly, helped by visiting religious and cultural events; during these days I also had the time to read. Christel is going home with me on April 17th. Our journey home took us through the French zone, always along the Rhine, where the fruit trees in their blooming splendour from the April sun greeted us from both sides. We could still see a lot of peculiar things, left over from the war, in this landscape. I so enjoyed these holidays and was full of joy and gratitude for all the beautiful things I was allowed to experience again.

In anticipation of the coming summer, some working days can be taken much more lightly, which otherwise aroused tempers. It doesn't always go so smoothly in the laboratory - but there was usually a peaceful end to every day. I take part in a DRK (German Red Cross) course two evenings a week.

Pentecost brings us together with Tante Dorchen and Onkel Hans, who are extremely excited about our current home in comparison to their home in Kevaelar now. At the beginning of June, I went to Kevaelar very quickly for two days and got gooseberries there. I visit Oma Ciba, who is doing quite well again, in the hospital. June 18th - Mutti's birthday is great to get us all together, Christel is here from Frankfurt. What I would like to mention is a greeting for Mutti from Frau Hüttner from Gleiwitz, which comes as a flower bouquet from home. A lovely, thoughtful surprise.

This year, at the same time as Mutti's birthday, comes the 'announcement of the monetary reform'. Of course, this measure robs us of the last of our 'savings money'. On June 20th 1948, for a deposit of 60 RM each, only 40 DM are spent per head for the time being, the remaining 20 DM are to be paid again. This exchange was 1:1 - while all money above that is devalued 1:10; in detail, the devaluation provisions look even more powerful. In any case, there is hardly anything left for us after these devaluation procedures. What seems to be successful about the campaign is the following fact: Almost all everyday items and food of all kinds that have been missing for years are partly free to buy, partly managed with rationing. But the amount of money needed to buy these basics soon makes itself felt!

In the company, I get my salary in instalments, which, incomprehensibly, was unfortunately reduced. Under these circumstances, my sea voyage to Borküm had to fall through. This year's summer didn't give us nearly as much sun as last year, so the cancellation of the trip wasn't taken quite so badly. Even here in Bielefeld, I didn't go swimming this summer! A few things are also changing in the company: Theesener Strasse is moving back into the main factory, where we don't like the space and surroundings at all. But before we get used to some new things, a job change occurs. Only Miss Laubner stays in the laboratory. I go to Dr. Krametz in the advertising department to write advertising letters to the gentlemen doctors, and Mr. Ochlert is dismissed like many others. A lot is happening these days and everyone's sense of security seems to be faltering. The changes occurring are not a bad thing! Nevertheless, I take my remaining days off at the beginning of September 1948, coming at a really suitable time, and on September 6th I go to Frankfurt. The one-week holiday brings a lot of variety and puts me in a pleasant environment for a brief time. In Taunus

Forest and on the Main, I am experiencing this year's late summer in the autumnal, warm and bright colours. Cycled to six different places, visit the Rosenthal factory - porcelain manufacturing demonstration - in Bad Vilbel.

At the end of these days, there should have been a wine trip to Rüdesheim in happy company, which unfortunately was cancelled due to technical errors with the transport. When I return home, I learn from Yugoslavia that Wolfhart's journey home is imminent. A riddle with all sorts of tricky arithmetic that he set, is to be brought to us on the day of his journey home. Yes, this reunion after such an infinitely long time is, I think, eagerly awaited on both sides!

In October, we are still blessed with wonderful sunny autumn days - so providing for the winter has worked out quite well. We were able to harvest and make quite a lot. Worth mentioning in this month, a long-awaited visit from Dr. Kahlert, Bärbel, Tante Liesel and Oma Ottile (*Dr. Kahlert's mother*). Such beautiful hours of reunion fly by only too quickly!

A series of song recitals by the Black Sea Cossacks in the Oetker Hall on October 18th, 1948, gave me particular pleasure. Under the conductor Boris Ledkowski – an impressive appearance – the singers introduced the secrets of an unexplored land in the East. Cossack Dancing!!

Again, a change is approaching in the company that will bring all sorts of things with it. It is the 15th November when the new "Disassembly List 2" will be released. We hear the news with trepidation: All female academics, some doctor's assistants, other employees and workers have now met the fate of dismissal. I had all sorts of worries and headaches for this change, especially since my new boss, Dr. Krametz, let his secretary influence me in a very strange way. But everything went well for me, while Dr. Krametz was stuck in another place. My letter-writing activity is pleasantly interrupted by frequent laboratory work, to which I am called from time to time. So, there is a lot of variety towards the end of the year, which, yes, will bring a long-awaited surprise: Wolfhart's homecoming!!!

Christel was with us for her 22nd birthday and spent a whole week with us. Yes, it's nice when we can be together again, every day - we also have all sorts of things to discuss about the Christmas preparations. On 4th December, we spend a pleasant afternoon with Günther Heller, a dear visitor from Gleiwitz.

He came with news of what I had secretly hoped for over the last five years. Suddenly it is to become a reality! On 6th December 1945, a telephone call from Wolfhart, who is already in the homecoming camp in Münster, really gets me into the pre-Christmas joy. Yes, our first meeting should build a bridge over all the past five years.

Wolfhart writes in Ursula's diary.

December 17th 1948. This day, which, in 1943, was our farewell day, is the day when the bridge is built, from that day to this, over five long years, full of misery, hardship and deprivation. The wise providence and the goodness of our great God have made this day a holiday for us; and not just a holiday, but a day of thanksgiving for everyone who has survived.

18th - 23rd December 1948

The days were filled with joy, understanding and concern for the welfare of the human being who had finally been found. Today, on the last day of my stay here, I would like to express my heartfelt thanks to you, dear Ciba family, for the love and kindness with which you have surrounded me, with which you have made my days a happy experience.

Yet this is something more than just an everyday occurrence. So, we want to bow before the omnipotence of our great God and thank Him, because we must be grateful to Him for our survival and existence. When this day ends, we will be separated by hundreds of kilometres, but only spatially, because the great bridge will connect us, hour by hour, over the bastions and evils of the world, a bridge that human feet have never crossed.

I wish your dear parents, you, dear Uschi, and your sister a blessed and happy holy Christmas and a hopeful coming year. So, I say goodbye with the deepest thanks to your dear parents and greet you, dear Uschi, from the heart.

Wolfhart Pesler, 23rd December 1948

So, we have seen each other again, in good health - and we were so full of joy and deep gratitude for this gift. What will the future hold for us? Will we be allowed to reach the goal that everyone desires, even if it must be kept very secret?

1949 and 1950
A visit from dear Fräulein Erdhütter, and we spend some pleasant hours together at the beginning of this new year. She is extremely impressed with our new 'home' although there is still a lot to do.

As far as my job is concerned, laboratory work always alternates with the science department, where I found particularly lovely employees with whom I worked well.

After the experience with Dr. Krametz, Dr. König, in his calm, balanced manner lets me breathe deeply. It didn't take long before Dr. König left the company and worked in his newly established practice in Jollenbeck. Dr. Krametz followed as department head for a while, then Dr. Jäger and finally Dr Gerlich, the previous head of the scientific department - exciting events happen all the time, but over time we have learned to face them with indifference. Several have been able to successfully look for another job themselves, others have left. In these difficulties, the collective bargaining with the trade unions is taking place and, years late, we are now getting the salaries that have not been properly calculated up to now. I'm not going on vacation this summer; I'm preparing for a change. I've already made such a start in the spring (journey to Münster) and finally my departure from Wolff is planned for later this year. With a tear in my eye, I left familiar surroundings, especially as far as the research work in the laboratory was concerned. But on the other hand, I can also say, with a twinkle in my eye, that I have a lot of desire and eagerness to start my new phase of life, which should bring me much joy.

So, on 4th October 1949, I travel to Frankfurt am Main. Here was a fresh start for me with regard to continuing my education because I hadn't made any progress since my studies in Breslau. Leaving home wasn't that easy!!!! From a financial and time point of view, I was not able to continue in Breslau and decided - always interested in medicine - to do physiotherapy.

I chose Frankfurt, where I wanted to study the four semesters, because I was moving to where Christel was, so found a piece of home right away. Of course, it hasn't always been easy, for those who have previously earned their own money, to be on a rather small budget. This problem can be overcome through a job placement with the express student service. At this point I was able to use shorthand and a typewriter for various assignments to improve my financial situation. I was happy to be learning again, in both an academic and practical situation. I met some of my old colleagues from working at Wolff, who were also in Frankfurt for a term of study.

After Christmas holidays, Jochen was with us from the seminary. He gave up the baker's apprenticeship in September 1949, after taking exams, and went to the seminary for the priesthood in October 1949, where he went through lectures at a rapid pace to finish his A levels and it seems to have all worked out well for him.

A lot has happened for Christel since Christmas - she always falls on her feet, she is an incredibly lucky child.

I'm going home alone at Easter. Christele goes with a friend to Rothenfels on the Bürg. I spend my birthday in 1950 at home. With laboratory acquaintances from Wolff, Miss Dr. Ackersmann and I have the same birthday, we have a small celebration.

This year, I hear nothing from Wolfhart for my birthday; our relationship has obviously suffered from all sorts of sad events that happened after we were together. This development is quite strange when you think of everything that has happened so far - his visit in December 1948, in particular. It is my hope everything will be fine one day!!!!

During the second semester, spring 1950, we experience the approaching summer and then finally in all its high summer fullness – visiting the beautiful beaches, paddling in boats on the Main, or swimming early in the morning. Tours by bike are made - short trips to the Kahler Lake or along the Rhine to Eltville-Kiedrich, Bonn and St. Goarshausen. The weeks leading up to the semester break are fast approaching and I was looking forward to spending a short holiday together with Christele. We wanted to go to Borküm. But she didn't pursue the matter with the necessary verve, and, because of her lack of interest, it didn't work out. So, I went home, but I wasn't that happy, because I already knew from letters what had happened there - Oma Ciba, who had come to the 'fruit festival' at Pentecost this year, had had an accident in the city and was with us, lying in plaster with broken ankles. Jochen stayed with us for the holidays, he was supposed to earn some money with holiday work. The house was full, my vacation was cancelled so, accordingly, I only had the tiniest space

I could use - we called it 'the visitor crack!'. There was plenty of work to do with pickling the cucumbers and cabbage and with guests in the apartment, it was always busy, so my free time went quickly. Despite the disappointing circumstances, I didn't take the time at home too badly. Christel had eventually settled for a holiday on Chiemsee (Bavarian Sea); yes, suddenly she managed to do it and now there was no way we could travel and experience things together as I had planned. When she returned to Frankfurt, all sorts of things happened, Christel was often on official business with George Trimming, interpreting for the regeneration of railways project run by the British and Americans. On the road for a few days at a time, the news of her from home was sometimes unbelievable; I, however, was still striving for the realisation of my silent longing!

At the end of October 1950, Christel moved to Munich, still working for Mr. George Trimming as an interpreter. I stayed alone, which I found difficult at first. Now every worry and every concern fades away for her, as it does here, too. In the middle of November, I spend some time in Bielefeld with my parents. Oma is at last well again and back in Kevaelar.

Shortly before her 24th birthday, Christel is in Frankfurt for a few days with work. And a few days later, my longing becomes reality - I travel to Italy.

Having saved my money, and planned this for over a year, I made this pilgrimage, with other people who had been expelled from their homeland in Upper Silesia, on 28th November 1950. I could think of nothing better, to celebrate being 25 years old, than to visit Rome - the Fatherland of my soul - and there, to look back, giving thanks for God's protection, blessings, power and grace during the difficult years gone by and to ask for the whole world to know His love and to live in peace.

Epilogue

*U*rsula became a physiotherapist, living and working in Frankfurt. Her relationship with Wolfhart came to an end in circumstances that are unclear, although I did find a photograph of his marriage in Ursula's things, so it seems they remained friends, for a while, at least. She never mentioned Wolfhart by name but, with a wistful smile, acknowledged there had been someone special in her life. Ursula never married, which gave her the freedom to travel widely, Italy being her real love. She inherited her father's appreciation of finesse and quality with an eye for fashion, design, culture and architecture. She would only wear clothes made from cotton, linen, wool or silk which were often handmade for her, just as they had been in her childhood. In 1979 she did travel, with her Mutti, back to their Heimat in Gleiwitz, now Gliwice in Poland. My mother could not bring herself to go with them. However, during that visit, Ursula collected some earth and grass from Gleiwitz which she kept in two labelled glass vials. We found them when we cleared her flat and sprinkled some into our mother's grave as we laid her to rest in November 2020.

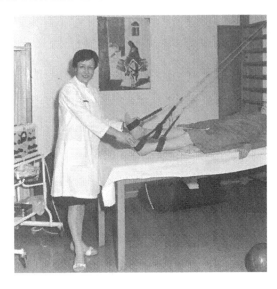

*M*y mother came to England in July 1951 and began a new life in London as a bi-lingual secretary. She met my father, Bernard George Cross at a New Year's Eve party 1952/53 at Brompton Oratory, Kensington, hosted by The Newman Association. As a game, guests had to mime a children's nursery rhyme for others to guess the title. 'Sing a Song of Sixpence' proved a little tricky for a young German woman, so the gallant Bernard George stepped in to help. And so began the next chapter of her life. Married in Bielefeld, Germany on 21st April 1954 they began their married life in Guildford, Surrey, where Michael was born. A job with the Beecham Pharmaceutical Company meant a move to South Africa where Margarete, Monica and I were born. Following a transfer to Copenhagen, Denmark, where Barbara was born, we returned to England in 1963. My mother kept her German passport, never became a British citizen and although a regular visitor to her Mutti, Vater and Ursula in Bielefeld and Frankfurt, she never went back to Gleiwitz.

There may have been no way home to Gleiwitz for Christa-Maria;
in the end, Gleiwitz came to her.

The End

Christa-Maria and Ursula in 2006, celebrating Christa-Maria's 80th birthday.

Appendix One: The Journeys Travelled

------- Ursula   ------- Christa-Maria   ///////// Sudetenland

------- Family   ——— Area of The Greater German Reich in 1939

Christa-Maria's Journeys in 1945 - a total distance of approximately 2,420km. The current names of places which are now in Poland or Czech Republic are in brackets. Polish names are written in bold.

November 1944 - Gleiwitz (**Gliwice**) to Wahrenbrück RAD via Dresden-480km.

April 1945 - Wahrenbrück to Gamnitz (Jemnice) in Czechoslovakia (Czech Republic) - 640km.

Via Rühland, Dresden, Aussig (Ùsti nad Labem), Karlsbad (Karlovy Vary), Marienbad (Mariánskê Lâgnē)and Plan (Planá) crossing border from Germany into Czechoslovakia (Czech Republic)

June 1945 - The Trek

Gamnitz (Jemnice) to Ditfürt - 615km.

Via Lichtenstein (Lištany), Anischau (Únêšov), Tepl (Tepla), Theusing (Touzim), Bad Gishubel (Boži Dar), Teplitz-Schonau (Teplice-Sandov), Deutscheinsiedel, Mulda, Nossen, Riesa, Leipzig, Aschersleben, Quedlingburg, Ditfürt - a journey from Czechoslovakia (Czech Republic), through forests and over the Eastern Ore mountains, back into Germany.

December 1945 - Ditfürt to Gera –164km.

December 1945 - Gera to Bielefeld – 520km.

Via Arenhausen and Ahlen, a journey crossing from the Russian zone in East Germany to the British zone in West Germany. The Ciba family made this journey together, after they had been reunited in Gera.

Map credit: Personal archive.

Ursula's Journeys in 1945 - made with her parents, a total distance of approximately 1,070km.

August 1945 - Gleiwitz (**Gliwice**) to Gera – 550km.

Via Oppel (**Opole**) Görlitz (**Zgorzelec**), Löbau, Ebersdorf, Pützkau, Dresden, Glaüchau, Gera.

Der Landrat zu Freiberg
--Der Dreierausschuss f.d.Flücht-
    lingsfrage --

Freiberg, den 2.August 1945.

A u s w e i s

für Flüchtlinge aus der Tschecho-Slowakei.

Name: *Grita Ciba* ....geb.am *28.11.1926*
Beruf: *Ahinrichtin* ....bisheriger Wohnort: *Gamnitz*
Ehefrau geborene: ....
Zahl der mitreisenden Kinder: ....
Der Grenzübertritt erfolgte in **Deutscheinsiedel**am: *22.8.1945*

    Die oben Genannten haben sich nach Mecklenburg zu begeben.
Sie haben folgende Marschrichtung zu wählen: Deutscheinsiedel-
Neuhausen – Sayda, von da mit der Bahn bis Freiberg. Von dort
weiter mit der Bahn nach Mecklenburg. Im Flüchtlingslager zu
Freiberg kann 1 Tag gerastet werden. Den Flüchtlingen gewährte
Verpflegung ist .... zu vermerken.
    Die Marschrichtung ist unbedingt einzuhalten. Dieser Ausweis
ist bei jeder Anfangsstelle vorzulegen.
        Im Auftrage:
        R ü h l e m a n n .

An vorstehende Personen sind Lebensmittelmarken (bezw. Verpflegung) für
folgende Tage: *23 b. 24.8.45* ... in *Freiberg* **Lagerleitung**
    "   " ... *25.Aug.1945* ....in ....
    "   " ....in ....
    "   " ....in ....
    "   " ....in ....
    "   " ....in ....
    "   " ....in ....
    "   " ....in ....
    "   " ....in ....

Flüchtlingen   Registrierungskarte   Karte Nr. *60732*

1. Name: *Ciba, Christa Maria*   2. Geschlecht: *W.*
3. Staatsangehörigkeit: *D.R.*   4. Alter: *19*
5. Von wo: *Gamnitz O.S.*   6. Beruf: *Schülerin*
7. Ärztlich untersucht
  a) Krankheit: 8a) Religion: *R.*
  b) Überwiesen: b) Durchgang:
8. Desinfiziert: c) verpflegt bis: *23.8.45*

N. B.: Diese Karte soll bis zu Ihrer nächsten Verfügung in Ihrem Besitz bleiben.

Christa-Maria's travel pass allowing her entry into Germany after The Trek from
Gamnitz in Czechoslovakia.

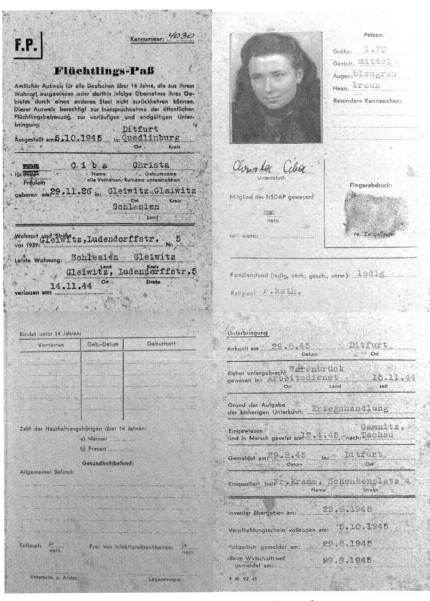

Christa-Maria's refugee pass issued in Ditfürt.

Der Oberbürgermeister der Stadt Gera

— Abteilung für Familienunterhalt —

Name der Verwaltung

— 28 mm —

Tagesstempel der
Gepäckabfertigung

Nachweis Nr. _____

für

_____ kg Gepäck zu Gepäckschein Nr. _____

von _____ *Gera* _____ nach _____ *Eisenach* _____

über _____ *Ohrenshausen* _____

Aufgeber 2) _____ *Ciba, Arthur* _____
                    (Name, Stand)

275

G u t s c h e i n Nr.

über

4 Personen

28 RM *50* Rpfg

Tarifentfernung *213* km 1)

Die Gepäckfracht ist auf Antrag und zu Lasten de _____
Unterzeichneten gestundet worden.

_____ *Gera* _____ , den _____ 20.12.45.

Die umrahmten Teile sind
von den Eisenbahnstellen aus-
zufüllen.
1) Wenn durchstrichen (im
Verkehr mit bestimmten Pri-
vatbahnen), Gepäckfracht nur
aus dem Tarif ersichtlich.
2) Die Angabe des Namens ist
freigestellt. Bei Gutscheinen
für mehrere Personen können
die Namen auf der Rückseite
vermerkt werden.

Gutschein über Gepäckfrachtstundung

Unterschrift

(Stempel des
Stundungsnehmers)

The Ciba Family's travel pass from Gera to Bielefeld, December 1945.

Appendix Three: Photographs

Martha Halamuda (1866 - 1930)

Martha Halamuda was born in 1866 and married Josef Jurettko, a post man, in 1888 in Gleiwitz, Upper Silesia, Germany. Martha was widowed in 1898, aged 32, when Josef died of a lung infection. Josef was just 36 years old. She lived in her apartment on 20, Wilhelm Strasse, Gleiwitz until her death in 1930, aged 64.

1900.

Joseph Jurettko.

1930.

Martha's Children.

Paul Leo Jurettko (1889 - 1937)

Paul moved from Gleiwitz to Breslau and became a medical doctor. In October 1925, he married his partner after she had divorced her first husband. They had a son, Günter, in January 1926. However, their marriage was short-lived, and they divorced in May 1930. Paul and Günter were regular visitors to their family in Gleiwitz until 1937 when Paul died in Breslau. Günter was 11 years old.

It was many years before Ursula and Christa-Maria saw their cousin again.

1898.

1910.

With Ursula in 1926.

Josef Ernst Jurettko (1890 - 1946)

Josef lived in Gleiwitz, working as a salesperson before becoming an accountant in later life.

1899.

1911.

1941.

He married Elisabeth Albertina (Elly) Frank on 23rd October 1917 in Gleiwitz. They had one son, Jochen, in 1931. Tante Elly's parents were Adalbert Frank and Elisabeth Gritz.

Alfred Karl Jurettko (1891 - 1915)

During World War One, Alfred served in the German Navy on the SMS Karlsruhe 1. He survived when this ship sank after an internal explosion while attacking commercial shipping lanes near Barbados on 4th November 1914. Alfred and one hundred and forty-five other survivors were taken back to Germany via Norway on the SS Rio Negro, arriving on 6th December 1914.

The following year, Alfred went on a tour of duty as a radio operator in a submarine, U30. He died on 19th June 1915, just days before the U30 returned to port on 22nd June 1915. The exact circumstances surrounding his death are unknown. He is buried in Evangelische Lutheran Cemetery, Auricher Strasse, Emden, Lower Saxony, Germany.

Sadly, there are no photographs of Alfred.

Bundesarchiv, DVM 10 Bild-23-61-01 / CC-BY-SA 3.0.de.

History	
German Empire	
Name	Karlsruhe
Namesake	Karlsruhe
Builder	Germaniawerft, Kiel
Laid down	1911
Launched	11 November 1912
Commissioned	15 January 1914
Fate	Sank 4 November 1914
General characteristics	
Class and type	Karlsruhe-class cruiser
Displacement	Normal: 4,900 t (4,800 long tons)
	Full load: 6,191 t (6,093 long tons)
Length	142.2 m (466 ft 6 in)
Beam	13.7 m (44 ft 11 in)1
Draft	5.38 m (17 ft 8 in)
Installed power	14 x water-tube boilers

Margarete Franziska Jurettko (1894 - 1993)

My Oma was born in Gleiwitz and lived there with her mother, Martha. She worked as a telephone operator. When not at work, Margarete helped to look after the lodgers who stayed at their apartment. After the war, she and Artur made a new life in Bielefeld. When Artur died in August 1969, she moved to Frankfurt am Main where she lived with Ursula at 23, Städel Strasse, in a third-floor apartment, until her death in September 1993.

1903.

1917.

1984.

Artur Josef Valentin Ciba (1895 - 1969)

1950.

1957.

Jochen Jurettko (1931 - 2004)

After his work as a baker's apprentice and time in a seminary for the priesthood, Jochen became a newspaper journalist. He had one son, André. Seen below left, Jochen, with his parents at his First Holy Communion, Gleiwitz, March 1941.

1949. Left to Right -
Opa (Artur Ciba), Oma (Margarete Ciba),
Ur-Oma Agnes Ciba, Jochen and Ursula.

Tante Dorchen (Dorothea Herbst née Ciba) 1920 (1898 - 1974).

Hans Herbst 1970 (1894 - 1974).

Adolf Ciba 1930 (1862 - 1934)   **Agnes Ciba** 1935 (1872 - 1957).

He worked as a load master on the railways.

Curate Wensel Schenk (1913 - 1982).

Wensel Schenk in 1975.

Wensel Schenk studied Theology at Breslau University (Wrocław, Poland), was ordained a priest by Cardinal Bertram in 1938 and became a close friend and spiritual guide of the Ciba family in Gleiwitz. It was Curate Schenk who looked after the photo albums in 1945, from which some of the photos in this book are taken. He went on to become Monsignor Professor Dr. Schenk, specialising in liturgical history.

Appendix Four: Recipes by Margarete Ciba

Spitzkuchen

500 gr. Mehl
100 " Rübenkraut (Sirup)
100 " Honig
100 " Zucker
40 " Fett
1 Ei
8 gr. Pottasche
4 " Hirschhornsalz
1/2 Teelöffel Zimmt
1/2 " Kadamom) gemahlen
1/2 " Nelken

Rübenkraut, Honig, Zucker und Fett werden erhitzt in die wieder abgekühlte Masse gibt man die Gewürze und verknetet alles mit dem Mehl und den übrigen Zutaten. Pottasche und Hirschhornsalz werden in lauwarmen Wasser aufgelöst. Aus dem gut gekneteten Teig formt man 4 cm dicke Rollen backt sie ab und schneidet noch heiß Dreiecke, die mit Schokoladen- oder Zuckerguss bestrichen werden.

Wünsche gutes Gelingen.

Pfefferkuchen

1 # Honig (Bienen oder Kunsthonig)
1 # Zucker
1/2 # Margarine
2 ganze Eier
2 Eigelb
1/2 # süße Mandeln (grob gehackt)
1/4 # Zitronat
1/4 # kleine Rosinen, 3 Esslöf. Kakao
2 1/2 - 3 # Mehl
2 Päckchen Neunerlei Gewürz - Pfefferkuchengewürz
2 " Triebkraft oder 2 Backpulver

Honig Zucker mit 4 Eßlf. Wasser heiß erlösen nach kurzem Abkühlen mit den anderen Zutaten vermengen. Zum Schluß das Mehl, Gewürz u Trieb-kraft vermengen bevor durchkneten. 1/2 Stunde kaltstellen, ausrollen und erst eine Probe backen. Zerlaufen die Formen noch etwas Mehl einkneten. Einen Teil des Teiges kann man als Platte ausrollen mit Marmelade bestreichen und eine 2te nicht zu dicke Platte darauf legen abbacken und noch warm in Würfel schneiden. Die gebackenen Pfefferkuchen mit Schokoladen- oder Zucker glasur bestreichen.

Elisenlebkuchen   46 half quantity

5 ganze Eier
3/4 # Puderzucker
1 # Haselnußkerne ungeröstet durch die Handmühle drehen
1 Teelöffel gemahlene Nelken
1 Messerspitze Zimtkaneel
1/4 # Orangeat
1/4 # Zitronat
50 gr. Aprikosenmarmelade
geriebene Zitronenschale
1 Prise Salz

Eier u. Zucker ganz cremig rühren bis eine dickflüssige Masse entsteht. Mit den anderen Zutaten gut zu einem glatten Teig vermischen. Auf runde Oblaten - 6 cm im Durchmesser - streichen und 3 Stunden trocknen lassen. Danach die Elisenkuchen bei guter Mittelhitze 15 Minuten backen. Nachher mit Schokoladenglasur bestreichen und Hagelzucker draufstreuen.

References

'Aftermath : Life in the Fallout of The Third Reich, 1945 - 1955', by Harold Jähner.

'Cultural Borderland in sociological and political perspective : (the case of Upper Silesia)', by Szczepański, Marek S. 1999.
https://rebus.us.edu.pl/handle/20.500.12128/9879

'The Gleiwitz Incident', by Dennis Whitehead.
https://www.docdroid.net/Z7hZb3D/after-the-battle-142-the-gleiwitz-incident-pdf

'The last days of Gleiwitz - January 1945',
Article by Marian Jabloński 2015.
https://www.24gliwice.pl/wiadomosci/ostatnie-dni-gleiwitz/

'Gleiwitz : A local storybook', by Rudolf Schlegel.
https://www.google.co.uk/search?q=Rudolf+Schlegel+Gleiwitz%3A+A+local+St ory+book&ie=UTF-8&oe=UTF-8&hl=en-gb&client=safari#vhid=GhEJ4rSl2Cp-fM&vssid=l

'The Death March from Auchwitz'.
https://auschwitz.net/deathmarch/
https://encyclopedia.ushmm.org/content/en/timeline-event/holocaust/1942-1945/death-march-from-auschwitz

'Memories of the end of WW2: A dangerous journey to Quedlinburg', by Hans-Herbert Biermann, 2015.
https://www.mz.de/lokal/quedlinburg/erinnerungen-an-das-kriegsende-im-harz-eine-gefahrliche-reise-nach-quedlinburg-2031154

'Expelled into the future: New Home, old fears',
Article written by Katrina Kaufmann, 2021, for the public German radio and TV broadcaster Nord Deutscher Rundfunk (NDR)
https://www.ndr.de/geschichte/chronologie/Vertreibung-nach-Kriegsende-Neue-Heimat-alte-Aengste,fluechtlinge7022.html

Glossary

Booty	useful items found in bombed-out buildings.
Christa-Maria	variously referred to as Christele, Christel, Kitta.
Featherbed	an unsectioned bed covering filled with feathers and down.
Frau	Mrs.
Fräulein	Miss
Heimat	homeland, its culture and traditions
Herr/ Herrn	Mr.
Kaffee und Kuchen	German tradition of having coffee and cake in the afternoon.
Kreis	region, similar to a county in UK.
Kreutzkirche	a church in Gleiwitz, attended by the Ciba family.
Mutti	mother.
Onkel	uncle.
Pfefferkuchen	a biscuit or traybake made with a mix of honey, citrus rind and spices, including cinnamon, cloves, nutmeg. Baked, decorated and eaten at Christmas time.
Reich	empire or realm.
Sisterlein	a mix of English and German to convey affection in a greeting to a sister.
Schlepp	to drag or to haul.
Streuselkuchen	a traditional German cake or pastry known for its sweet crumbly topping. Variations can include adding apples or cherries to the base or mixed spices to the topping.
Tannenbaum	tree/ Christmas tree.
Tante	aunt.
Ursula	also referred to as Uschi.
Vater	father.

Acknowledgements

My siblings, Michael Cross, Margarete Isherwood, Monica Hosie and Barbara Cavanagh for agreeing to let me write this book for our family and for their support and proofreading.

My children, Bronwyn Alsop, Duncan Ainsworth, Fabienne Bennett and William Ainsworth for their love and support while I have been absent with my head in an iPad.

Joe Alsop at Alsop Design, for the family tree and map.

Matthew Bird, for typesetting and getting 'No Way Home' publish ready.

Franz Kahlert, who provided letters written by my Oma and Opa (Margarete and Artur Ciba) and shared his recollections about Gleiwitz.

Maria Kahlert, who gave permission, on behalf of her family, for their names to be used in this book.

Fellow authors from Michael Heppell's 'Write that Book' Masterclass Alumni, in particular: Elaine Wallace, Judith Lisgarten, Samantha Hawkins, Mark Rogers, Penny Chamberlain, Debra Murphy, Charmaine Host, Jane Geffin and Erika Beumer for their encouragement, advice and support.

And very importantly, I want to thank Jim Dunleavy, who has been so understanding, made endless cups of tea and dinners for the last nine months and has been there when I needed a hug. Thank you for being there. ♥

About The Author

Elisabeth Dunleavy lives in UK cruising the waterways on a narrowboat, ChristaBella.

A mother and grandmother, she felt compelled to bring this story to life. After several years of research, personal recollections and translating the diaries, she has written this memoir.

It is her debut work.

Printed in Great Britain
by Amazon

30054671R00151